WHAT SNOWFLAKES GET RIGHT

OXFORD
UNIVERSITY PRESS

Oxford University Press is a department of the University of Oxford. It furthers
the University's objective of excellence in research, scholarship, and education
by publishing worldwide. Oxford is a registered trade mark of Oxford University
Press in the UK and certain other countries.

Published in the United States of America by Oxford University Press
198 Madison Avenue, New York, NY 10016, United States of America.

Library of Congress Cataloging-in-Publication Data
Names: Baer, Ulrich, author.
Title: What snowflakes get right: free speech, truth, and
equality on campus / Ulrich Baer.
Description: New York, NY, United States of America :
Oxford University Press, [2019] | Includes bibliographical references and index.
Identifiers: LCCN 2018061167 (print) | LCCN 2019010909 (ebook) |
ISBN 9780190054205 (updf) | ISBN 9780190054212 (epub) |
ISBN 9780190054229 (online content) | ISBN 9780190054199 (cloth : alk. paper)
Subjects: LCSH: Academic freedom—United States. |
Freedom of speech—United States.
Classification: LCC LC72.2 (ebook) | LCC LC72.2 .B34 2019 (print) |
DDC 378.1/213—dc23
LC record available at https://lccn.loc.gov/2018061167

9 8 7 6 5 4 3 2 1

Printed by Sheridan Books, Inc., United States of America

WHAT SNOWFLAKES GET RIGHT

*Free Speech, Truth, and
Equality on Campus*

ULRICH BAER

CONTENTS

PREFACE

*Disentangling the Free Speech Debates
in the Age of Trump, the Alt-Right,
and Campus Protests*

Free speech is woven into the fabric of our society, starting with the political protests against the Stamp Act in 1765 that led to the formation of the United States, the ratification of the First Amendment in 1791, the extension of speech rights to all Americans in later amendments, and finally our era when free speech seems to be in need of defense. America rests on the principle that we, the people, have a right to express our opinions without fear of official retribution. We can criticize the powers that be, scream our dissent at any politician we want, and argue for even the most outrageous ideas without danger of the government punishing us. But just as our country and our Constitution were born out of raucous debate that resulted in a compromise of many competing interests, the exact contours of free speech have remained a matter of heated argument. This is an altogether good thing: by leaving open where the line should be drawn between one person's right to speak and everyone's right to equally participate in speech, the Founding Fathers allowed this concept to serve our evolving nation remarkably well.

In recent years, free speech has emerged as a flash point in American public life under conditions the Founders could hardly have imagined. While personal insults pushed the bounds of acceptable discourse in politics, Chelsea Manning and Edward Snowden posted state secrets on the internet. Were these acts of bravery based on any citizen's right to dissent, or treason? When Colin Kaepernik and other athletes took a knee on the gridiron, was this a quintessentially American exercise of First Amendment rights, or an un-American dishonoring of our country's ideals? When people demand to be called "differently abled" instead of any other term, "undocumented" instead of "illegal," "pro-life" instead of "anti-choice," or insist on the pronoun "they" in the singular rather than "he" or "she," is this reasonable? Or is it politically correct policing of everyone's God-given right to speak any way they want? When activists record police actions and post them online, are such recordings protected expression, or violations of the officers' right to do their jobs without interference? Is donating money to a political campaign a form of protected speech? Is it permissible to use racial epithets in a workplace, or a graphic screen saver on your office computer? Can a baker be compelled to make a cake for people whose lifestyle he considers a violation of his religious beliefs? Is the government suppressing speech when it removes information about climate research from official websites, or when it prohibits language on abortion in federally supported health clinics? Should you be allowed to burn a cross in your neighbor's yard? On your own property? What about burning an American flag?

These issues cut across legal, political, and cultural considerations. Not all of them involve the First Amendment, and not all of them can be resolved by our courts. But few of them have generated as much confusion and angry conflict as controversies over speech on campus. Such controversies do not involve all of the legal and philosophical questions concerning speech. Indeed, many legal experts believe that the First Amendment is not the correct lens through which to view or resolve these conflicts, not even for public institutions. But campus controversies are instructive for anyone wishing to defend our personal liberties in a strong democracy based on equality. They foreground the complicated and inextricable link between freedom and equality in the university setting, which exists for a specific purpose. This purpose is the advancement of knowledge, which must be based on respect for the truth and the inclusion of all views based on merit rather than an individual's identity. Instead of just prompting you to be *for* or *against* free speech (neither of which is a philosophically coherent position), campus speech controversies are instructive scenes, or teachable moments, because they take place in an organization set up to create equality among otherwise very different people. While the university is not a political organization, this commitment to equality to which all members agree creates an instructive parallel to democratic life.

"We are not born equal; we become equal as members of a group on the strength of our decision to guarantee ourselves mutually equal rights," wrote political theorist Hannah Arendt. In a university this is the right to participate on equal terms. What to do when speakers don't respect the truth, dispute established facts, and undermine this commitment to equality that undergirds the university and, in a different way, democracy itself?

If a speaker and protesters both use their right to speak, who is to decide which side must back down (if either one does), and who is left with the right to speak and be heard without interference? Where is the line between robust exchange and interference at a university? Where is the line between controversial statements, vile opinion, and incendiary hate speech on campus? Should a speaker be permitted to spew hate, when students are restricted from posting the same language on a fellow student's door? Should the university allow *more* speech than other public institutions, even when such speech does not respect the truth, denies established facts, and fails to contribute to the advancement of knowledge or education?

These questions are no longer only intramural concerns that pit students against the older generation, in a pattern as old as education itself. The campus controversies are battles over who gets to decide what counts as the truth, what are proven facts, and what is expertise. First and foremost, these controversies are not about the First Amendment, or anyone's inherent right to free expression. They are about power: the power to privilege one right over others, the power to dictate what gets studied and taught, the power to determine how language works in specific contexts. They are as much about written rules and legal decisions as about norms of behavior. Most significantly, they are not about offense and resilience, nor about victims and winners. What makes the campus controversies so explosive is that they are as much about how we frame these issues, as they are about a specific situation. At a time when democracies are under threat around the world, political leaders dispute proven facts or ignore and dismiss the opinions of experts as elitist, the campus speech controversies are not about the hurt feelings of the students, whom former U.S. Attorney General Jeff Sessions dismissed, in 2018, as a generation of "sanctimonious, sensitive, supercilious snowflakes." They are about listening to the next generation's deep commitment to our country's original values, and about strengthening rather than severing the link of free speech and equality that is fundamental to our democracy.

Some of the responses on all sides of the speech debates are a distraction, to be sure. This is only natural when deeply held beliefs and legal abstractions clash with lived reality. It is all the more true when the younger generation is instructed to accept, without questioning, that free speech has been an immutable legal concept in our country since its inception, that the current legal definition of it is the best possible approach, and that merely voicing a concern about the fairness of this status quo amounts to an act of treason. This is, in a nutshell, the message of liberal and conservative self-styled free speech absolutists in response to anyone who questions current legal rulings and social orthodoxy: students will come around to see the wisdom of our courts' definition of free speech, even in situations, such as private universities, where the courts will not render a decision. They will grow up to learn that protecting hate speech and virulent racism, while regulating other types of speech for different legal reasons, is the best way to protect our democracy.

But the students have to come to understand something else as well. They have learned that the legal definition of free speech has changed over time, and that the history of jurisprudence shows that both the court's and the public's definition of free speech are not a static matter. They have also learned that allowing racist speech to flourish does not always flush it out of the country, but that protecting hate speech can also embolden hate groups to act with impunity. They draw attention to the fact that the Trump administration has broken with a decades-old tradition of moral leadership when the president fails to condemn the message of hate groups as un-American, while asserting their legal right to free expression as a fundamental American right.

In the wake of the events in Charlottesville, it has become more evident that hate speech cannot be simply defeated with more speech. It has also become more evident that defending an absolute principle of free speech only works for everyone when the principle of equality is defended vigorously at the same time. Defending free speech as an absolute right, without also rejecting the content of virulent racist and misogynist speech, creates a moral vacuum. It turns free speech into a weapon for a partisan agenda, rather than a neutral principle that serves all equally well. The adage commonly attributed to Voltaire, that I will defend "to the death" your right to say that which I abhor, makes sense only if you indeed state your disagreement. Otherwise, condoning someone's right to speak, purely on principle, looks like endorsing the speaker's message. Should the citizens of Charlottesville defend the neo-Nazis' right to their death? In light of the terrible events of August 2018, we probably do best to retire what has always been a vapid, misattributed line. In a decision rendered in 2018, Supreme Court Justice Elena Kagan warns against turning the principle of free speech into a weapon for a partisan agenda: "And maybe most alarming, the majority has chosen the winners by turning the First Amendment into a sword [...] The First Amendment was [...] meant not to undermine but to protect democratic governance [...]."

The risk identified by Kagan of weaponizing the First Amendment, which is a possibility for any fundamental law, is also found in the campus controversies. She cautions us not to turn the law into a one-sided weapon. This means recognizing the university's role in instilling respect for the facts, for evidence-based knowledge, and for the truth, rather than blindly asserting that being subjected to challenging ideas, even when it involves the circus act of unqualified provocateurs, automatically leads to understanding. Banning any speaker, even those with no academic qualifications or whose views have been debunked, the thinking went, threatens our democracy in more fundamental ways than allowing even the most vile and incendiary speaker to get a hearing. What if those speakers incite speech controversies to undermine the university and democracy itself? Kagan reminds us that free speech can become weaponized to undermine other principles. In the university, such a weaponized conception of free speech, which people often summarize as free speech "absolutism," can undo the university's commitment to equality and its central purpose of advancing knowledge and respecting the truth. Ironically, free speech absolutism can lead to a wholesale attack on the truth and on facts, which freedom of expression, in Jefferson's and Madison's conception, is supposed to protect.

The challenge of upholding an abstract principle of free speech, without inadvertently condoning the speaker's message, became apparent in the wake of Charlottesville, when President Trump chose not to condemn the white supremacists unequivocally. Up until hours before the deadly violence, and even after students at the University of Virginia had been physically attacked by right-wing protesters, conservative and liberal commentators had insisted on an abstract right to free expression even for the Ku Klux Klan and neo-Nazis. But this commitment to free expression was expected to be paired with a strong condemnation of these group's hateful, vile, and un-American messages. President Trump echoed this kind of free speech absolutism. Then he failed to condemn the speakers unequivocally while defending their right to speak. The resulting controversy revealed the difficulty of maintaining a commitment to free speech as an abstraction that does not become an endorsement of the message. In legal terms, such viewpoint neutrality is a cherished principle. In the academy and real life, as President Trump's remarks showed, such abstractions do not really work. Defending an abstract idea of speech, without considering the content and context of the speech, does not work outside of the law. The events of Charlottesville, then, are perhaps less about free speech then about violence, intimidation, and terror.

Liberals and conservatives may use the same words but have different understandings of what free speech means in specific contexts. Why do white supremacists and right-wing agitators choose college campuses to hold their rallies? They would surely get a bigger audience if they held their rallies in public parks, or rented out a stadium. Clearly, they do not mean to win an argument on academic grounds, but to score a symbolic victory. This, of course, is the nature of political speech, where the truth is important, but the impact on an audience often matters more.

Campus controversies bring clashing principles into conflict. The aim of establishing the truth, to which the university is committed, collides with a given speaker's wish to gain legitimacy for his message. This is also what Charlottesville was about: to legitimate and reopen a question that America settled as an undisputable bedrock principle and guiding promise at its founding. The alt-right does not respect and in fact openly disdains and disparages the university, but it wants its prestige and legitimation. They attack the press as enemies of the American people but expect the same press to provide accurate coverage, and, through this coverage, to validate their views as just another part of genuine public debate.

The alt-right and related groups ignore and openly attack the ground rules of academic discourse, including the absolute prohibition of incitement and deliberately demeaning speech, while expecting the university to grant them a stage based on a free speech principle. These groups have a history of intimidation and incitement, none of which is permitted in a university setting (similar to other public and private settings that enforce rules of conduct). They don't accept other points of view presented by speakers with equal standing, since their message is that some of those speakers are inherently inferior. But the university, whether public or private, upholds the principle of equality alongside free expression, and not in opposition to it.

To put the point more sharply: Should equality be a debatable principle? Or is Jefferson's notion an absolute value and non-negotiable precondition of social interactions, in addition to being our nation's law, to which all Americans must consent? The university powerfully illustrates the absurdity of putting equality up for debate, because academia depends on and is legally required, per Title VI of the Civil Rights Act of 1964 and Title IX, of 1972, to guarantee equal participation of all of its members to fulfill its mission. If we debate the conditions of speech in this way, we turn the concept of free speech against itself. In this way, the university's dual commitment to equality and free speech can teach us something about how a democracy of free and equal citizens works .

Free speech controversies are battles not chiefly about a correct interpretation of current First Amendment jurisprudence, which has limited application in the university, as many legal experts agree. They are not so much about our fundamental rights as individual citizens, even though the issue seems to turn on one person's right to say whatever he wants in any setting. They are also not primarily about the feelings of a generation, which, according to those who draw lines between appropriate and inappropriate modes of disagreement, is overly coddled. The campus speech controversies center on the role of the university as gatekeepers to reliable knowledge, and as *arbiters of truth* in a democracy. They are about the role of expertise in establishing the truth, and about the independence of academia, akin to that of an independent and free press which must not be forced to publish anyone's opinions, in determining what is worthy of debate. They are a conflict between an institution that values and protects ideas that serve the purpose of finding the truth, and the public that rightly values speech for additional reasons, because it is entertaining, provocative, or politically effective. A host of non-academic organizations provide considerable legal and financial resources to bring controversial speakers to college campuses. But the aim, in many highly publicized controversies, is not first and foremost to debate ideas. The provocateurs do not want to speak on campus only to hawk their books or to defend the First Amendment, even if they occasionally emerge as martyrs of this principle and gain support from all sides of the political spectrum, from the American Civil Liberties Union (ACLU) to the Goldwater Institute.

The speakers of our day seek the platform and prestige of universities because a college invitation functions as a tacit endorsement and legitimation of a point of view. It's a bit like having one's views accepted by editors for a major media outlet, or a book published by a reputable press with high standards. These speakers could easily present their ideas with a megaphone in a public park or online, which come closest to the notion of a largely unregulated marketplaces of ideas. In any public venue, where speech serves a different purpose than in a university, a speaker can reach many more people than a few hundred or, in extremely rare cases, over a thousand college kids. But speakers seek out the university because that is where some of the rules are made about what counts as legitimately established knowledge, and what ideas are simply bunk. It is this function of the university of vetting and legitimating knowledge, with the aim of winnowing truth from settled falsehoods, that makes the speech debates so important.

What gets discussed in universities and published in academic journals may seem arcane and utterly removed from real-world concerns. But this process establishes a truth according to norms and rules that value expertise and genuine debate over political and actual power. Of course even academia is not free of such matters, but its fundamental principle is not to let *power* decide what counts as reasonable and what is merely bunk. This is why the free speech debate specifically at universities deserves special consideration: it is a struggle over what constitutes a legitimate matter to be discussed by our society, and what is a crank idea that might flourish online but does not merit serious study and debate. Although the site of these disputes is academia, the matter is universal. It concerns the university's special role in a free and democratic society of finding a truth that is independent of raw power, namely through structured debate that is based on reason and evidence.

Even the most dramatic speech controversies are side shows compared with this deeper, more significant and consequential struggle over how to decide on what counts as true or false in public life. On the internet, few filters screen truth from falsehood, even if media companies also exercise their right to control content. In our current moment, when the news is regularly attacked as fake, and confirmed scientific findings are directly denied by political leaders, when ignorance and unreason can signal autonomy and independent thinking, as Tom Nichols diagnoses in his book *The Death of Expertise*, this role of setting guidelines for establishing the truth based on reason is the ultimate prize. Speakers travel to campus not to enforce First Amendment principles or to debate. Victory means simply going on stage, regardless of credentials or the academic consensus in any given field, since a campus visit means challenging the university's function in society of creating rules on how to determine the truth. What is presented as fighting political correct pieties, of which universities certainly have their share, is in reality an attack on expertise. Often, the campus controversies are also frontal attacks on America's foundational principle of equality, without which the idea of any individual's freedom of speech is rather meaningless. Here I draw chiefly on Catharine MacKinnon's incisive link of speech law and equality law, which proves indispensable for any serious consideration of the role of free speech in democratic institutions and society at large. What we need to disentangle in the speech debates are how the principle of free speech relates to academic inquiry, how the university's mission of advancing knowledge depends on the equal participation of all, and what assumptions underlie these separate but related processes.

In his visionary conception of a democratic republic, Thomas Jefferson insisted that education was the tool to guide the masses whom we rightly entrust with great political power, but who would tend to abuse such power unless properly educated. In the preamble to "A Bill for the More General Diffusion of Knowledge," Jefferson counseled that "the most effectual means of preventing [tyranny] would be, to illuminate, as far as practicable, the minds of the people at large." At a moment when public trust in the recognized arbiters of truth, namely serious journalism and science, is directly attacked by political leaders, this Jeffersonian purpose of education, of learning how to tell truth from falsehood in a society of free and equal citizens, seems all the more crucial. Like the media, publishing, and science, universities are in the business of teaching people, in ways Jefferson probably anticipated, how to distinguish between truth and lies, between verifiable facts and alternative realities. The framers feared a situation where raw power determined the truth, which means the basic political organization of our lives. Educating citizens and protecting their capacity for dissent are related projects; free speech was intended, by Madison and Jefferson, to lead to a better outcome for all—and not to protect ignorance, falsehood, and raw power masquerading as dissent.

A key dimension of this process is robust debate in the pursuit of knowledge. But this process is not a free-for-all where all ideas are included without any standards, and anything is up for debate. Our constitutional protection of free speech assures that individual citizens can voice political dissent without fear of punishment. At a time when the press and science are under severe attack, we must do everything to safeguard this principle. But for our efforts to be effective, we must clarify how free speech depends on an equally powerful notion of equality, and how the university invites robust debate for the sake of advancing knowledge. We must spell out how the principles of free expression, lawful equality, and respect for the truth are distinct but *interdependent* values in a free society. The campus debates serve as an important opportunity to disentangle these critical issues for our time.

FREE SPEECH AND

THE UNIVERSITY

What Is at Stake

THERE IS WIDESPREAD CONFUSION ABOUT the role of the university in regulating offensive speech. The speech debates on campus have been unhelpfully framed as a conflict between America's exceptionally broad and absolute conception of free expression, and overly sensitive students. The perception that results is that our constitutional rights are being sacrificed to spare the feelings of politically correct and coddled students who refuse to engage with controversial topics, or simply viewpoints with which they disagree. This idea should give even those partial to the students pause.

Indeed, nobody should be forced to compromise our constitutional commitment to freedom of expression because of hurt feelings. But such a choice is misleading. The speech debates on campus are not about destroying our Constitution for the sake of sensitivities. Instead, we are faced with tough questions about individual rights and speech that materially undermines equality guarantees on which the university, and our democracy, rest. But there is a way of disentangling these issues that does not force us to decide in favor of speech over equality. It is not only the case that a line can be drawn; in rare instances, a very narrow line *must* be drawn so that speech does not become a rigid abstraction that overrides the university's mission and, instead of supporting that mission, produces the exclusion it stands against.

Many people assume that in order to arrive at the truth, universities should allow any and all ideas to be openly debated, and that regulating speech flies in the face of this commitment to open inquiry. But recent campus controversies make obvious that the principle of open inquiry must be followed with a bit more nuance.

LET EVERYONE SPEAK

The need for clarity came into sharp relief after three people died and over 30 were injured in connection with a white supremacist rally in Charlottesville, Virginia, that followed a march and rally by the same people on the campus of the University of Virginia on the previous evening. The American Civil Liberties Union (ACLU), along with nearly all liberal and conservative media outlets, had defended the neo-Nazis' right to a rally in a particular area, from which the city had sought to move them over safety concerns. "The Jews will not replace us," several hundred people chanted while marching across campus, some sporting helmets, and many carrying tiki torches, guns, and batons. "Whose streets? Our streets!," they shouted. The price we have to pay for our rights, many commentators said before the rally, is to tolerate hateful, vile, and divisive chants. Defeat such speech with better speech, others said. But after three deaths, many serious injuries, and legal convictions for first degree murder, the white supremacists' invocation of their First Amendment right to march on campus begins to look like a weapon to destroy our cherished principles, and not a necessary instrument to ensure open and robust debate.

In remarks after the event, President Trump appealed to the principle that we must allow all perspectives to be heard. He condemned "hatred, bigotry and violence, on many sides," and, after an outcry from politicians and pundits across the political spectrum that he had failed to condemn the neo-Nazis, clarified the statement in which he had identified "very fine people" among the alt-right. While President Trump's phrasing was folksy rather than philosophically nuanced, and while he sought here as in other instances to dismantle a politically correct idea, the president echoed what commentators of all political stripes had said a day before the deadly rally. Everyone is entitled to express his or her opinion regardless of how foul or vile, free speech absolutists had insisted. The university, where the alt-right held the first rally, must host speakers from all sides, including neo-Nazis and the Ku Klux Klan. The legal concept of "viewpoint neutrality" should regulate our attitude toward speech in all contexts. We should maximize speech from all perspectives, since knowledge is never complete and today's errors may prove to be tomorrow's wisdom. Then the president's comments, although they echoed this content-neutral stance toward speech, were condemned by commentators and politicians on all sides. What had changed? When the nation's leader declined to place virulent racist ideas beyond the pale of acceptable *political* discourse, his defense of the white supremacists' *legal* right to speak, which free speech absolutists have invoked after each campus controversy, suddenly looked not like defending an abstract constitutional principle but like condoning and endorsing the speakers' views.

NO SIMPLE ANSWERS

After the carnage in Charlottesville, it became evident that the battle over speech on campus is not necessarily a matter of sheltering sensitive students from controversial views. The violence tragically highlighted that these situations, which have roiled many campuses, are not simply resolved by invoking abstract principles. The principle of absolute speech rights that override all other concerns, to which the president alluded in his comment, "on many sides" without condemning one of these sides, is of limited use when having to make actual decisions in a specific context.

Often, the challenge amounts to resolving a volatile situation on the ground where legal solutions do not provide all of the answers, but moral leadership is required. In my roles in the university and through in-depth conversations with leading experts and students at a range of institutions, I have learned that there are not always simple answers, and that in most cases, all sides on the speech debate wish to make not only important but indispensable contributions to the community. When a student group issues an invitation to an incendiary speaker, either in the belief that the speakers share their commitment to reasoned debate, to challenge what they view as politically correct sensitivities, or to introduce these ideas into a wider forum, high-minded appeals to jurisprudence are of limited help. When another group protests such a choice, they also act in the belief that they are defending the university's commitment to truth and reasoned debate. For the first group, equality is a matter of debate; for the second group, equality is the non-negotiable condition of debate. The question is: Is this really a choice? Or does the university compromise its very mission and purpose, which is something the courts have always recognized as worth defending, when allowing one principle of absolute speech rights to override another one, of equal participation?

While the Supreme Court's decisions structure our public debates and to some extent guide everyday behavior, it has become obvious that regulating speech only after violence has occurred leaves universities dangerously exposed. If legal rulings could never be challenged, and if the courts were also the legislators, it would be akin to living under totalitarian rule, rather than the rule of law. This is why the courts regularly hear new cases and revise earlier rulings, based on their best interpretation of foundational texts and our laws. But there is a way of unpacking these issues, even if they seem intractable at first glance. It is possible to draw a line between what speech must be permitted, and which ideas do not merit debate in the university. This can be done without compromising either the university's commitment to equal and unfettered debate, or our nation's laws and principles.

IT IS NOT A MATTER OF OFFENSE

To do so, we need to understand that the key issue in these debates is neither offended feelings, nor is it political correctness. In fact, the framing of these issues as matters of political correctness has become misleading ever since that term has become shorthand to ridicule those who advocate full equality in the university setting. Although the media frequently highlights angry students, their emotions are not central here. Neither are safe spaces, speech codes, and trigger warnings, which are far less prevalent at our nation's roughly 1,700 public and 2,500 private two- and four-year colleges, than news stories would imply. Safe spaces have existed for as long as modern universities have offered gathering places for students of a non-dominant faith, for instance a Catholic center or Hillel, or dormitories segregated by gender. Speech codes are meant to regulate behavior just as rules regulate conduct in any workplace, and it is an open question whether attacking such codes on legal grounds truly benefits the university's functioning. The presumption in any attack on speech codes, trigger warnings, and safe spaces is that there was once a status quo prior to such rules that was natural and Edenic. But universities are, in their essence, a community's voluntary submission to rules that promote certain goals. The fear is that any new regulation, such as trigger warnings, speech codes, or safe spaces, *worsens* the existing state of affairs. The question is not whether rules should exist. Rather, the idea is that new regulations will exacerbate rather than alleviate distortion because of wrong motives. Let's be clear here: trigger warnings, speech codes, and safe spaces are intended to afford all students, and especially minorities, equal learning opportunities. Their intent is not censorship, as is often asserted in the hunt for motives. But their motive is indeed political, as many critics of such rules insist. Equality concerns are always political. The debate is whether new rules improve or worsen the status quo, or whether not changing the rules leaves intact the comforting illusion that until quite recently, universities had no rules at all, or that the rules of yesteryear worked perfectly for everyone.

Even speech absolutists recognize that posting hate symbols on a particular student's dorm room door crosses the line from free expression to incitement. Taking into consideration the impact of disturbing content before screening it in class, for instance a graphic video of human pain and suffering, is commonsensical behavior. Indeed, an early proponent of trigger warnings is Aristotle, who warned that excessive exposure to cruelty can dull our moral faculties. There are countless controversial topics debated in colleges around the nation on a daily basis, without resulting in press coverage and charges of constitutional decline. Many challenging curricula question reigning orthodoxy according to academic protocol. The fierce debates over what constitutes an appropriate curriculum have long been part of university life. There is no simple answer when students challenge the selection of texts, and there is no inherently neutral, static position from which to proclaim some texts to be unacceptable, or useless, and others indispensable. The students are entitled to an explanation of why certain texts matter (which is the very point of teaching), just as faculty are entitled to choose what they teach. When students deploy the same bullying tactics they decry in conservative agitators, their behavior is unacceptable. But they certainly have a right to an explanation of the rules, rather than be told that adhering to existing rules, which had not been designed for many of them, serves them best. What's changed is that today's students can amplify their voices via social media, while previous generations battled for their rights on different terrain.

But the tactics of students are not directly equivalent to those of people with institutional power. They are by definition in a position of dependency on the faculty who grade them. It's not that they are correct by dint of their social standing. My point is that such debates cannot be simply decided from an objective position that evaluates each claim as if made in an institutional and moral vacuum, where everyone speaks from identical places. The students draw attention to the fallacy of such an assumption, and alert us to the fact that power must be included as a factor in any analysis. They also express impatience, which is often the province of the young, with anyone who says the status quo and its rules are fine, the university works well for everyone, and nobody has a right to complain. We need to see that in some of the controversies, an overly rigid and abstract principle is deployed to promote speech that materially undermines the university's functions, which depend on the equality of participation and informed respect for expertise. Instead of trying to resolve these scenarios after the fact, once they have become volatile and even deadly, it is possible to lay out some ground rules that protect both speech and the university's mission.

DIFFERENT RULES FOR DIFFERENT SPEECH?

In a discussion of the role of free speech on campus, Addis Fouche-Channer, a student then in her final year at Middlebury College, where a controversial speaker's visit resulted in violent protests, questioned why campus speech rules seem to differ depending on the speaker:

> Middlebury would never bring a climate change denier because that just doesn't fit in with our values, and our thought

process, and what we know to be true. Middlebury would never bring a Holocaust denier because that just doesn't fit with our values, or our thought process at all. So when you bring in somebody [like Charles Murray] who's going to challenge the well-being and the humanity of a lot of people on campus, that just proves that Middlebury isn't a safe space for everyone in the way it appears to be.

We find a deeper explanation and implicit response to the student's question in an interview between journalist Bill Moyers and Professor Joan Scott, a distinguished and judicious historian formerly at the Institute for Advanced Studies. Discussing various incidents over speech on campus, Professor Scott reluctantly makes a case for inviting a white supremacist to campus in the name of free speech:

> I would have a hard time banning even Richard Spencer from speaking on a university campus, however hateful and dangerous I find his ideas.
>
> [. . .]
>
> Moyers: What's the difference between a climate denier and a Holocaust denier?
>
> Scott: I think not much these days. I think not much at all because the climate denier tries to prove, as the Holocaust denier does, that the facts that demonstrate that there was a Holocaust and that there is climate change are wrong and don't exist—against all evidence that they exist.
>
> Moyers: Should a professor be able to teach creationism in the biology curriculum if half the students believe it?
>
> Scott: No. Absolutely not.
>
> Moyers: Why?
>
> Scott: Because, again, we're talking about what counts as science. If the students don't want to learn about evolution, they shouldn't be in the course. A biology course that teaches

creationism is not a science course, it's a religion course. So the
students demanding that creationism be given credence in that
course are out of line and are denying the academic freedom of
the professor. They are calling into question the scientific basis
of the material that's being presented. And students are not in
a position to do that.

How do we account for this gap in the attitudes toward
speech? The student identifies an inconsistency in attitudes
toward speech, when colleges allow racial pseudo-science
on campus, in the name of free speech, but deny a platform to speakers who deny established facts. Are today's
students abandoning the guarantee of personal liberty? Are
an alarming number of people under the age of 30, as some
commentators argue, giving up on the Constitution for the
sake of harmony? Do the students inappropriately put their
feelings above reason, according to those who decide which
feelings matter and that it is possible to think without the taint
of affect? The student, in fact, does not invoke hurt feelings
but points out an inconsistency in the university's definition of what counts as worthy of debate. Are there indeed
different rules for different kinds of speech? The professor's
recommendation is that noxious ideas, including virulent
racism, should be subjected to open and robust debate lest
they fester underground. The denial of facts that are a matter
of the historical record, and not a matter of opinion, such as
the occurrence of the Holocaust and climate change, by con-
trast, does not deserve a campus platform. But what looks
like different standards applied to different speech, which the
student considers remarkable, is not an error or an inconsistency. By identifying this difference in the university's practical decision-making about which speakers are invited to
campus, both the student and the professor—although they

arrive at different conclusions—bring to light a core role of the university.

THE UNIVERSITY'S PURPOSE IS TO VET IDEAS

Every day, universities exclude some ideas from debate while inviting others. Before we look at *which* kind of speech gets invited, we need to understand that this vetting process in the university is not a secondary matter in the speech debates, but essential to everything we value in education. The student at Middlebury asks us to consider not only a specific instance but in more general terms how speech contributes to, and in what cases it undermines, the university's mission. What is this mission, and how can speech interfere with it, rather than always contribute to it? How does a talk by someone whose peer-reviewed and rejected argument about the inherent inequality of some racial groups figure here?

The university's mission is to teach students, often through the vigorous debate of a great range of viewpoints, and to conduct research that advances knowledge via open intellectual exchange. In practice, this means the testing of old ideas, the presentation of new ones, and the open-ended exploration of entirely novel questions based on verifiable evidence. Students are trained to learn these procedures, the goal of which is to find the best solutions to a given problem. The aim is to establish the truth, not as a matter of blind faith in a given hypothesis, but via a consensus of experts in a relevant community who have studied an issue in depth. But the point is to advance knowledge, and not just to discuss whatever comes to mind. The result is a convergence of evidence-based findings, for instance that germs can cause disease, that Thomas Jefferson fathered children with the enslaved Sally Hemings, or that left-handed children are as capable as right-handed ones. Once the truth has been established by considering the evidence, it becomes a paradigm that guides further research, both as a methodology and as an implicit set of accepted ideas. Often skeptics remain, as there are about the proven fact of Jefferson's African American children, or about the broad expert consensus that HIV causes AIDS. But at some point, the community of experts has accepted some facts as settled opinion, and moves on to discover new things within this paradigm. Skeptics are largely ignored in serious academic debate, for instance the historians who dispute Jefferson's relationship with Sally Hemings, since to discuss their denial of proven facts does not advance knowledge.

The point is not to establish an inviolable, eternal standard of "the Truth," and to dismiss all other viewpoints as heretical. But the objective is to reach agreement, based on available evidence and accepted methodologies, on the truth as a baseline for further research. The goal is to establish the truth not by institutional authority, force, or clever rhetoric, but through a cumulative and collaborative method that guards against bias and unseen error. The debates to reach this truth are often contentious, and within academic disciplines factions form around different viewpoints. While teaching often means examining a given paradigm closely, and sometimes to address skeptics, robust and open academic inquiry and exchange do not mean that any idea can be re-introduced willy-nilly into the debate. Once scholars have accepted a set of facts by reaching a consensus, for example the theory of the Big Bang, the reasons for the extinction of dinosaurs, or the financial situation of France at the time of the Louisiana Purchase, it is included as an indisputable ground rule for proceeding. The range of examples can be expanded greatly to show that the exclusion of some ideas as outright silly or absurd is standard procedure but that people tend to make absolutist exceptions when it comes to racial pseudo-science.

In the university there is a great amount of research into knowledge for its own sake, which means that even the presuppositions of established facts are routinely examined. But while all facts may continue to be hotly debated and disputed in the public sphere, where everyone is entitled and encouraged to express even counter-factual opinions freely, in the university setting, the validity of some facts, except as part of a clearly defined pedagogical exercise, is no longer subjected to unfettered debate.

SPEECH SERVES A SPECIFIC FUNCTION IN THE UNIVERSITY

For this reason, the best analogy to the university is not the public park or some areas of the internet, where anyone is allowed to express nearly anything, but the halls of Congress or a courtroom, or perhaps a town hall, where individual voices carry enormous authority but speech must follow clear ground rules in the interest of reaching a shared goal. In the classroom, the research lab, and the lecture hall, students are not free to discuss anything they want, and faculty are not free to teach falsehood and lies. In the university, the goal is pushing the boundaries of knowledge in the interest of advancing the truth.

The same principle applies when universities decline to host speakers who present novel sightings of the planet Vulcan between Mercury and the Sun, dispute the existence of gulags in the Soviet Union, or promote intelligent design as a viable scientific alternative to the theory of evolution. None of the decision to exclude speakers with such viewpoints, many of whom would love a university invitation, conflict with any law or violate the First Amendment. The rejection of such speakers also does not compromise the university's commitment to open exchange or to hosting a broad range of views. So far, this seems commonsensical. If the university allowed all conspiracy theorists to promote their crank theories, it would not be a university. Students would be exposed to many ideas, but they would not learn that the process of searching for the truth has its own rules, instead of being a free-for-all.

Then why does a university's decision not to host a white supremacist ignite a nation-wide controversy, activate the ACLU, and prompt countless pundits, liberal professors, as well as the nation's president, the attorney general, and the secretary of education to attack universities, call for withholding funding, and agitate against politically correct students? Why are virulent racists defended in the name of free speech principles, while the daily and routine decisions not to invite a hobby astronomer for a lecture, and to restrict students in a history class from discussing last night's baseball game, barely register in the public eye?

To understand this difference, the example of intelligent design is instructive. Creationists have long used First Amendment doctrine to insist that their views must be taught in schools. In the 1925 "Scopes Monkey Trial," in Tennessee, lawyers had argued whether states have the authority to direct the teaching of evolution in publicly funded schools. The widely publicized trial, and its media coverage, convinced large parts of the public to accept scientific expertise, rather than public opinion or religious belief, to set the curriculum in schools. In subsequent trials, our nation's courts have viewed intelligent design as a religious concept that conflicts with the establishment clause, which prohibits the government from imposing a particular religion via its institutions, as it would do if intelligent design were taught as science in public schools. What is important for our question about speech on campus is that to arrive at its ruling, the court relied on the academic consensus of experts and on science, rather than public opinion or faith, to clarify a matter of public concern.

But even after court decisions and scientific consensus, the public will often continue debating topics that academia has settled. The notion of innate racial and gender inferiority was laid to rest by many scholars, including the evolutionary biologist Stephen Jay Gould in *The Mismeasure of Man*. Biology departments do not teach racial pseudoscience, such as phrenology, and history departments teach it only as a social artifact, but not a valid theory. The notion of innate inferiority never died on the internet, where speech is largely unregulated. It has now come back into the university through campus visits by speakers who argue that white Americans are inherently superior and therefore deserve more rights in our country. Such opinions do not merit careful examination. In 2018, a giant of modern science, James Watson, who identified the double helix structure, was discredited and stripped of his honors by the laboratory he led because of his unscientific racist views. The laboratory did not engage a commission to examine these views but considered them beyond the pale of what merits further debate. But here we see how a free speech argument can be used to get around the university's normal and everyday screening mechanisms. The constitutional scholar Fred Schauer calls this "First Amendment opportunism," when the principle of free speech is used in inappropriate contexts to dislodge other procedures by which speech is regulated to fulfill specific purposes.

The notion that women cannot attain "[M]an's higher eminence . . . in whatever he takes up," as Charles Darwin put it in *The Descent of Man* (1871), where he placed the imprimatur of science on gender inequality, is discussed in today's universities only for its historical and sociological worth, but not as a valid scientific theory. No science curriculum denies the difference between men and women, but no science department in a credentialed university teaches that women are innately inferior and men superior, rather than just different.

The issue of racial and gender inferiority, and the persistent claim that some people are not fully human, will concern us throughout this discussion. It touches on the legal and moral value that must be reconciled with the idea that no speech must ever be regulated, which is our pluralistic and diverse country's non-negotiable commitment to political, legal, and social equality.

THE DIFFERENCE BETWEEN EXPERT CONSENSUS AND THE PUBLIC SPHERE

The point is that universities rely on expertise to *routinely* exclude some ideas in order to function. They screen out obsolete or false ideas, or what experts consider settled debates, even when such ideas do not conflict with legal rights concerning religion, as had been the issue in the Scopes trial, by relying on experts. This is why *The Protocols of the Elders of Zion*, a fabricated anti-Semitic text meant to look like a real historical document, is not studied as a primary source in history departments but only as a hoax, identified and considered as such. None of these content-based exclusions of speech constitute punishment or unconstitutional suppression of speech. By not subjecting mermaids, the idea that September 11 was an inside job, or that Barack Obama was not born in America, to robust and unfettered academic inquiry, universities do not create an "echo chamber of political correctness and homogeneous thought," which is the phrase used by former U.S. Attorney General Jeff Sessions when he criticized universities during a visit to Georgetown Law School in 2017. The Attorney General used a deliberately broad brush to obscure the difference between discussing ideas that merit expert scrutiny in order to advance knowledge, and discussing ideas that prove popular but play no role in teaching and research, or actively undermine the university's functioning. In fact, universities maintain the culture of vigorous debate to weed out unseen error by filtering which ideas are fit for discussion. This vetting process is the university's precondition of using speech to advance knowledge.

The same principle applies in the classroom, even if students are not yet experts in a given field. For teaching to occur, students accept that the ideas introduced into the discussion must contribute to a better understanding of the issue at hand. If a student wants to discuss an unrelated matter, or revive a long-settled and obsolete idea, such as women's inferior capacity for abstract reasoning in a physics class, or the existence of light-bearing ether, she is not always permitted to continue but may instead be referred to the existing literature. When a student is told not to continue discussing certain things, this does not mean that her First Amendment rights have been violated. The teacher has the authority, and indeed the obligation to exclude ideas not germane to the topic at hand, without breaking any laws. What *is* required by law, however, is that the teacher ensures that all students can participate in the discussion on equal terms.

ROBUST DEBATE, BUT IN THE SERVICE OF ADVANCING KNOWLEDGE

Someone might object that we should let the marketplace of ideas, not a faculty member or administrator, separate useful ideas from nonsense. This confusion is at the heart of many arguments about academia, including the attacks on the university by self-appointed watchdog groups that rank colleges on "viewpoint" diversity and the presumed censorship of some ideas. It is connected to the attack on experts as inherently elitist, and on the dismissal of established facts as fabrications and fake news. The suspicion of expertise, to be sure, has a long history: it dates back to Plato's fear of a tyranny of the truth over people who should think and make up their minds for themselves. Today's conspiracy theorists do not share Plato's realization that while the truth can become tyrannical, the completely unregulated promotion of ideas, for instance in the form of public opinion, can also become unbearable.

To cut through this dilemma of respecting expertise but not letting a cabal of stodgy professors determine what merits debate, some recommend, like Professor Scott, that in some cases it is better to debate offensive and even incendiary views out in the open. This corresponds to Supreme Court Justice Louis Brandeis's notion, as he phrased it in an often-cited 1913 *Harper's Weekly* article, that "sunlight is said to be the best of disinfectants." Unless all and even nonsensical ideas are introduced into open debate, how can we be sure that professors won't just confirm their viewpoints in a politically correct closed loop that shuts out new ideas?

But there is an essential difference between subjecting the academic consensus about a given topic to informed scrutiny, and insisting that universities must host all speakers at any time. By taking this latter tack, the campus debates are often framed as a problem created by politically correct students who cannot handle ideas they judge offensive. Several organizations have made it their mission to combat what they consider liberal "groupthink," and to ensure that all ideas, but especially those *they* define as unorthodox and controversial, which almost always tend to be about race or gender, get fair discussion time in college. These self-appointed watchdog organizations frame the important issue of speech on campus as a one-sided, valiant defense of reason, and of a state of affairs with no speech regulation, against political correctness and hurt feelings. They confuse the critical role of expertise, and of evidence-based reasoning leading to consensus, with the exercise of censorship. They plead for unfettered speech rights in their defense of rationality. But they tacitly slip in telling qualifiers when describing the university's method as "reasoned" argument, or, in the words of Professors Robert George and Cornel West who have issued a high-minded appeal to free speech as an absolute value, as engaged in "truth seeking." These words, "reasoned" and "truth seeking," are far more than simple adjectives that clarify the self-evident idea of absolute freedom of expression. They echo the qualifiers used in a series of Supreme Court decisions, dating from 1919 and 2014, that invoke the marketplace of ideas "in which the truth will ultimately prevail" and where "the best test of truth is the power of the thought to get itself accepted." Of course the justices know that thought, in and of itself, has no agency to prevail and "get accepted." But they choose not to examine the age-old conflict between truth and politics already central to Plato. They do not engage with the philosophical tradition that ponders the relation between truth and power from the Greeks to Thomas Jefferson, Hannah Arendt, Judith Shklar, Michel Foucault, and legal theorists such as Kimberlé Crenshaw, Mari Matsuda, Charles Lawrence, and Richard Delgado. In so doing they side-step a historically and politically informed understanding of how power functions in establishing the truth in a marketplace of ideas that is not a static, empty, and abstract thought experiment.

These terms prompt rather than resolve the question that ignites many campus controversies: How can the university advance knowledge, via reasoned discourse, when it hosts speakers who promote unreason and blatantly disregard and dispute the validity of scientific methods, fact-based evidence, and the truth? How can a university promote "reasoned" argument and "truth seeking" discourse, when the speaker's point is to deny the power of reason, deliberately deny proven facts, and disregard the truth?

THE UNIVERSITY AS AN ARBITER OF THE TRUTH

It is surely important to hold academic disciplines and universities accountable and keep them from lapsing into dogma. This is all the more critical under the complex conditions of our globalized world, when information is ubiquitous, communication instantaneous, and proven facts are at once openly denied by people in positions of authority and, strangely, also assumed to speak for themselves. The idea that a guild of initiated experts in a few institutions topped by ivory towers, who are protected by life-time tenure and perhaps quite aloof, can decide what a media-savvy public in a pluralistic society should think about, seems arcane and contrary to a new openness that pervades the world. Isn't it better to allow anyone to join the academic debate, and then decide, once they have had a spot in the lecture hall, whether their ideas have any merit? The reality of a group of academic experts and administrators reaching consensus strikes many people as the outmoded rituals of an unhealthy and self-referential cabal, rather than a dynamic and open process of serious give and take that will guard against unseen error.

But the idea that colleges must host any speaker, regardless of qualifications, the importance of his or her views, or the relevance to the overall mission of advancing knowledge, obviates the university's very purpose. If the university allows anyone who wants an invitation to mount a stage and present his or her views, including the deliberate denial of proven facts, it renounces its chief purpose of deciding which ideas merit debate, and which ideas do not. It abandons the expertise which differentiates the university, including public institutions, from the public sphere, and which constitutes its very reason for being. For some time now, both pundits and our nation's leaders, including the president and the heads of federal agencies, dispute established facts, disparage or dismiss anyone who offers evidence they do not agree with, and openly eschew scientific expertise. These attacks on expert

equality. Is equality a principle open for debate, or is it a non-negotiable premise and true bedrock of our society?

Today, universities are sued and threatened with the loss of federal funding when they decline to provide a platform to any notoriety-seeking mountebank. Tomorrow, they will be sued when the medical school declines to host a privately funded speaker who denies the health risks of tobacco, when the science departments do not appoint a faculty member who disputes the environmental costs of burning fossil fuels, when the law school declines to host someone who argues against judicial autonomy, or when the college does not hire someone who argues that women should not go to college but stay in the home, or that slavery had been good for the enslaved. Indeed, well-funded efforts exist to impose conservative political viewpoints on the curriculum at various universities. These efforts are made in the name of fighting political correctness, liberal groupthink, and the alleged ideological corruption of the hallowed realms of teaching and research. But they blatantly undermine the principle of academic freedom, which aims at establishing the truth and not a particular ideological outcome, and which protects the authority of experts from political pressure. Why do we believe that a judge or legislator will have a better grasp than an academic of what merits academic debate? The constitutional right to free speech will be cited not to bolster but to undermine academic freedom of inquiry, which is the exercise of debating and using reasoned judgment and established expertise to advance knowledge, and not a free-for-all battle of opinions where the loudest voice can trump the truth. This is why every decision in this area has consequences outside of the academy. The slippery slope so feared by free speech absolutists can lead not only to governmental restrictions of speech, but has already led to governmental impositions via state legislatures of particular research and teaching agendas on universities. If the university is no longer permitted to decide which ideas merit academic debate, its crucial role as one of society's arbiters of truth is put at risk.

THE IDEA OF VIEWPOINT NEUTRALITY

Many people hope to move past the controversy by citing the legal concept of "viewpoint neutrality." This technical approach is used by our courts, notably different from courts in many democratic societies around the world and different from courts during earlier periods in our country, in order to regulate speech in the public realm as an abstract vessel, regardless of content and largely divorced from the consideration of its effects. By not regulating speech based on its content, the courts protect against both improperly motivated governmental action and the distorting effects on public discourse that would occur if only one type of speech were restricted. The idea of "viewpoint neutrality" became a standard legal practice in the early 1960s. Today, the notion of viewpoint neutrality governs part of contemporary jurisprudence in the United States, where content considerations (what speech says) and the effects of particular speech (what results it can produce), such as inflammatory speech, were largely swept away in a 1964 Supreme Court ruling, *New York Times Co. v. Sullivan*, in favor of "robust, wideopen, and uninhibited" debate in the public sphere. Even after the *Sullivan* ruling, the Court continues to exempt some speech, including what it defines as "low-value speech," from this broad protection, on the basis of both content and consequences. This means that libel, treason, fighting words, deliberate falsehoods, obscenity, and incitement can all be regulated by the state to preserve the social order. It also means that the court permits the suppression of language "on abortion" in faith-based clinics which receive public funding, to cite an example where conservatives, many of whom consider themselves ardent speech absolutists, favor restricting speech, by law, of which they disapprove.

It is worth stressing this fact: the United States Supreme Court has always recognized the possibility of regulating speech, and has *always regulated* certain types of speech, without violating the First Amendment. To speak of the First Amendment as an absolute rule does not mean that no speech can ever be regulated, but that the restriction on speech is narrow. Even the free speech absolutists on the Supreme Court have ruled in favor of regulating certain types of speech. In such situations, and similarly with "low-value" speech, which is speech that the courts define as not contributing to social deliberation when it is spoken or heard, the state regulates the individual's right to free expression because this expression can threaten either targeted individuals, or the well-being of all, or makes no contribution to the greater good. While the definition of speech has been enlarged in recent legal rulings from mere speaking to include certain actions, such as campaign finance contributions and the baking of cakes, the Court has generally avoided making distinctions based on the content of particular speech.

The legal strategy of considering speech as an empty vessel, devoid of its content, seems to get around the challenges faced by universities. While there are a few exceptions for the types of speech that directly threaten the social order, universities—where robust debate is not only important but the very point—should follow the viewpoint-neutrality principle. Any other guidelines, speech absolutists maintain, go too far in restricting an individual's right to express his or her opinion. Fraternities should be allowed to sing racist chants; speakers should be permitted to denigrate individuals because of their group belonging. There is no "middle ground," as two experts on speech in the university, Erwin Chemerinsky and Howard Gillman argue, for any restriction even on vile speech that could lead to the suppression of potentially useful knowledge. While workplaces are governed by rules of speech and conduct, and the government has the right to penalize employees for inappropriate speech, the university should have the fewest rules for acceptable behavior. Even if a university tries to regulate speech that interferes with its core mission of expanding knowledge, aside from the direct incitement of violence, it must be legally stopped from doing so. Free speech absolutists place a dual burden on the university, all for the sake of advancing knowledge: it must be *more* open than regular workplaces to extremist language, and it must flush out and refute via debate, but never restrict, regulate, or ban, vile and false ideas. But speech regulation is the university's very business. And the university's right to conduct its affairs on its own terms, which are the terms of expertly guided debate for members on fully equal footing, is under attack. The *National Review*, to cite one prominent example, has published instructions on how to sue liberal arts colleges for multi-million dollar damages on such grounds. The Goldwater Institute authors legislative bills to penalize students who exercise their speech rights or protest against speakers in ways with which the Institute disagrees.

It is important to recognize that many of the lawsuits brought against universities, and the legislative bills calling for mandatory penalties and expulsion for demonstrating students, do not aim at protecting anyone's civil liberties. They also do not protect the category of political speech in content-neutral ways. Under the mantle of a specific interpretation of First Amendment rights, as instructions provided by the *National Review* make clear, these suits do not aim to expose students and other members of the university community to the greatest possible range of ideas. Rather, by centering on monetary damages, they aim to damage and undermine the university's key function as one of society's authorities on what counts as a fact, what is reliable knowledge, and what is merely hearsay, opinion, or belief. These targeted efforts to hurt colleges financially should be viewed not simply as valiant defenses of individual liberty, but as continuing the aggressive questioning of the purpose and value of a college education, the attacks on "tenured radicals," and the decades-long retrenchment of public funding for higher education. They hark back to Ronald Reagan's attacks on the University of California in his 1966 gubernatorial campaign, in the wake of the Freedom of Speech Movement fueled by demands for racial justice and equality, and extend to comments by Congressman Devin Nunes in 2018, that academia is an "enemy of the American people."

SPEECH SERVES A PURPOSE IN THE UNIVERSITY'S MISSION OF TEACHING AND RESEARCH

To understand this, we must recall that universities, whether private institutions that have more leeway about regulating speech, or public institutions that are government-funded, have a specific purpose or what the law calls "compelling interest." In order to fulfill this purpose, universities cannot use resources to underwrite activities that run counter to the mission of advancing teaching and research. As far as this fiduciary responsibility is concerned, universities do not differ greatly from other publicly funded institutions with a specific purpose, such as the halls of Congress, the reading room of your public library, or the local post office, where many speakers would not be granted the right to speak without any infringement of their civil rights.

Legal experts, including Mari Matsuda, Robert Post, Richard Delgado, and Stanley Fish, have argued convincingly that when a college chooses not to host all speakers, it is not violating any law. They have identified the difference between academic speech, which has the purpose of advancing knowledge, and free speech on a street corner. "First Amendment jurisprudence," Post, the former dean of Yale's Law School, explains, "is crafted to protect the political equality of citizens, which has little to do with the production of expert knowledge." By not granting every motivated speaker the same access to a college stage that we all have to a street corner as citizens with equal rights, universities uphold their obligation not to serve as the equivalent of a public park but to expand knowledge, without punishing anyone's speech rights. Post reminds us that the Supreme Court has ruled, in decisions dating to 1972 and 1981, that the First Amendment does not deny a university's "authority to impose reasonable regulations compatible with [the] mission [of education]," which includes "a university's right to exclude . . . First Amendment activities that . . . substantially interfere with the opportunity of other students to obtain an education." These views are part of a robust and long-standing debate among constitutional experts. The difference in the

Court's interpretation and application of First Amendment principles, and the fact that the Court has regularly voided or overruled previous rulings in light of new ideas, means that the First Amendment is neither a self-evident nor a self-enforcing law.

THE CONSTITUTION AS A GUIDE TO SPEECH ON CAMPUS

Other commentators insist that a particularly rigid interpretation of the First Amendment ought to be the exclusive standard for speech in the openly accessible parts of public universities, such as quads and plazas. Although American law has consistently recognized limitations on speech, and although these regulations of various types of speech in various situations have changed throughout time, these speech absolutists do not think that anyone can draw a line on what speech could potentially be relevant in a university. Erwin Chemerinsky, dean of the Law School at the University of California at Berkeley, yokes together legal principles and academic values: "The central principle of the First Amendment—and of academic freedom—is that all ideas and views can be expressed." But academic freedom precisely does *not* mean that all ideas *should* be expressed: it means that only those ideas are interrogated in academic settings that can play a role advancing the truth, which may exclude, for example, lies and proven falsehoods.

It is correct that the First Amendment embodies an absolute principle. The fact that this principle has resulted in widely divergent legal decisions and interpretations of the meaning and scope of speech, many of which contradict each other in key aspects, should be sufficient indication that "absolute" does not mean eternal, unchanging, and self-explanatory. Free speech decisions that had meant to serve as absolute standards have been regularly revisited throughout our nation's history, often been overturned, and have generated on-going legal and public debates. Even in the context of the law, the existence of an absolute principle does not mean that free speech means the same in all contexts. The term "absolute" here means that the principle of free speech does not depend on any other conditions to be true and valid but originates out of itself. It means that you must not question the validity, utility, and importance of free speech. But it does not mean that the meaning and application of free speech is self-evident, that we all agree on the best way of implementing and protecting free speech, or that even decades of legal rulings settle the debate once and for all. Differently put, the First Amendment is not identical to its current interpretation by our courts. It is not self-enforcing or static but like all laws, a rule that requires active and thoughtful interpretation. The fact that the Court has changed its approach to speech regulation over the decades means that an evolving society needs to regularly and rigorously interpret its laws, especially when they are of such importance.

The First Amendment serves as a guiding ideal, as the proud North Star of our nation's civil rights, in many people's estimation. But an absolute idea, while we rightly celebrate and defend it as an absolute, cannot be applied fully and absolutely in any human social context. Evidence of this fact is the vast and varied record of our Supreme Court's jurisprudence, which indicates that although free speech is an absolute principle and ought to be respected as such, it is neither self-enforcing, nor self-evident, nor can it be absolutely applied in all contexts in the same way. My point is to draw attention to the critical difference between the First Amendment as an ideal, and current legal interpretations of this ideal in specific contexts. Being a speech absolutist means defending the promise of personal liberty. But this defense of a principle may result in the vehement objection to current legal rulings made in the name of the First Amendment. Many commentators on the college controversies confuse these two things. When they say that hate speech is protected and must always be protected, and that viewpoint neutrality is the absolute standard to apply, they invoke a particular set of legal rulings dating to the 1960s, but nothing found at the core of First Amendment doctrine. The core of the Amendment says nothing about regulating libel, obscenity, defamation, treason, fighting words, low-value speech, deliberately causing a panic that can put people at risk, or any other category of speech that the courts seek to regulate. Defending the First Amendment means defending our best legal interpretation of this principle. It does not mean that the current interpretation is automatically the best of all possible interpretations. This kind of absolutism, which considers the current approach to speech regulation the best and only option, is indeed strangely intolerant of other views. It ignores the history of our country's jurisprudence and places current Supreme Court's rulings beyond debate, as if they were sacred and eternal truths rather than interpretations. But this kind of piety and absolute respect for any branch of government is exactly what the First Amendment should prevent. Saying that we can find better ways of enforcing the First Amendment means staying true to its core, rather than violating it.

The academic fields of critical legal and race studies, as well as feminist theory and other schools of scholarship on free speech, add nuance to the positivist legalistic view on free speech. They examine the law's role in both shaping and challenging inequality, and, via methodologies such as balancing, perspective-changing, and sociological approaches, interpret the best ways our laws should let everyone flourish in our democracy. Further proof of the fact that free speech is indeed an absolute principle but that this does not mean that it applies unvaryingly to human affairs everywhere, in addition to the record of our courts' legal decisions, lies in the history of philosophy. The pre-Socratics, Plato's account of the trial of Socrates for using speech to corrupt Athenian youth, to 17th-century English poet John Milton, America's Founding Fathers, Frederick Douglass, John Stuart Mill, Simone Weil, Hannah Arendt, John Rawls, and others, all acknowledge that free speech is an absolute principle, but that under specific narrow circumstances speech must be regulated for it to remain meaningful at all. If the principle of free speech were applied as an iron-clad rule to the university, by interpreting the framer's directive against governmental limits on speech as a stringent rule for universities, in order to allow anyone's opinion to matter equally, the university would have renounced its very function.

My point is that the significance of legal scholarship notwithstanding, the reliance on an abstract notion of the law, which has never been applied uniformly in all social contexts, is only of limited use. It is not helpful to equate a presumed essence of the First Amendment with current legal interpretations, and to insist that the current status quo is inevitably the very best approach of all. Indeed, the existence of legal debates is sufficient indication that free speech is a principle in need of interpretation. The application of an absolute and ahistorical conception of speech, which might be the legal status quo, to a static social space, rather than to the very specific context of the modern university, quickly becomes a purely academic and ultimately uninteresting flight from the concrete reality of life in contemporary America. This is the other reason university debates over speech are so important. Since they are built in large part to educate the next generation, today's universities are sites of a struggle over the nation's path. The changing demographic make-up of university students holds a mirror to America's future. If you visit a sufficiently broad range of American universities, colleges, and community colleges, and if you listen and engage with students, you can catch a glimpse of tomorrow. It is an evolving and dynamic space, rather than an abstract space fit for purely abstract debates.

The purist position on absolute speech rights is understandable. It is a powerful response to the threats to freedom of expression in our country today. This is the ACLU's argument, for instance, when its director, David Cole, warned liberals not to abandon the First Amendment after the election of Donald Trump, when all branches of government were controlled by one party. What Cole means, of course, is not the First Amendment but the current status quo in speech law. Deviating from this status quo, he fears, will cause harm to some. But what if deviating from the status quo, as the ACLU does when it challenges legal decisions based on speech law, improves America? What if the Supreme Court, as people with quite different approaches to speech issues such as Catharine MacKinnon and Erwin Chemerinsky have argued, has not always defended the rights of minorities and prevented the tyranny of the majority? What if things could be *better* with a different approach to speech controversies rather than worse? There is a very clear line between finding the correct interpretation of the First Amendment and challenging wrong-headed opinions, and abandoning the Constitution. If rethinking current legal doctrine would amount to abandoning America's founding documents, each and every justice of our Supreme Court would have acted against the Constitution. The Trump presidency should not cow us into accepting the status quo as the best possible situation at the moment, or prompt us to confuse the status quo, which is the way the law is currently interpreted, with the First Amendment itself.

Such an attitude ignores the best scholarship and practical knowledge gained over centuries. It also underplays our country's and our courts' contentious, complicated, and courageous history of arriving at a workable definition of speech at different times. It might lead to proclamations that may be intellectually satisfying and sound morally pure, but do little to sort out current debates. If you are a free speech absolutist, your first concern should be to make sure the First Amendment is interpreted correctly and not applied as an ahistorical abstraction to a static social space. If you are a free speech absolutist, anyone's warnings, whether by the ACLU or the Goldwater Institute, former Attorney General Jeff Sessions or former President Barack Obama, not to question whether the protection of hate spech is really the best interpretation of our laws, should concern you. I believe that universities can protect their mission as arbiters of truth without throwing open their gates to a rigid policy that happens to correspond to certain aspects of current legal rulings, but does not necessarily constitute the best approach.

IS SPEECH ABSOLUTISM THE ONLY ANSWER?

Beyond legal arguments, we need a clear account of higher education that is informed by what needs to be controversial on campus, for instance to unsettle dogma and stimulate new thought, and what puts an end to open debate. Students are confused and angry; faculty are torn; administrators are overwhelmed. Journalists are usually alarmed, sometimes because they conflate the campus debates over speech as attacks on freedom of the press. No reputable media outlet agrees to post just anyone's opinion without first vetting it; but no serious journalist believes that this vetting and editing process violates the freedom of the press, or anyone's freedom of speech. If news outlets can reject an opinion piece without violating the author's speech rights, why would universities be forced to host the same person based on speech rights?

Universities spend a great deal of money on speakers who end up with free publicity and some legitimation, while outside commentators fault universities, not without reason, for not following clear guidelines and letting things run amok. Even university leaders who cite absolute speech rights note that the university cannot host anyone who wishes to use the college campus as a platform. Legislators in several states have submitted bills calling for mandatory expulsion of student protesters. Various elected officials invoke speech rights to fault America's universities and threaten to withhold federal funding for not allowing completely unregulated debate. It is striking that only conservative viewpoints are so passionately defended as matters of free speech, even when this principle is called "absolute" and non-partisan. There are hardly any public discussions of Liberty University's removal of a visiting pastor, other conservative campuses' disinvitation of speakers with liberal views, or Harvard University's rescinding of the title of Visiting Fellow for Chelsea Manning in 2017. None of these incidents are mentioned by our nation's leaders as violating anyone's First Amendment rights. But given the complexity of each situation and the concern that one may inadvertently endorse a particular side, while the status quo seems to be perfectly neutral, it is tempting to join the self-styled speech absolutists by picking the simplest path: just letting anyone speak.

EQUALITY OF PARTICIPATION

While universities reserve the right to exclude some ideas from academic debate, they must not exclude individuals from participation based on non-academic principles. While a speaker may not be invited to lecture about the healing power of crystals in a medical school, or her studies of mermaids in the biology department, she cannot be excluded because she is a woman. A key dimension of the academic enterprise is that all individuals must be able to contribute to the discourse aimed at establishing the truth, regardless of group belonging. The operating assumption is that speech serves the purpose of winnowing the truth from falsehood, noise, and nonsense. The university's understanding of free speech assumes that anyone may have access to the truth, regardless of their particular identity. For this process to work, nobody must be excluded from the debate based on group belonging, including race, gender, ethnicity, national origin, sexuality, or similar traits.

While there is no academic reason for discussing the once-popular idea of the benefits of slavery for the enslaved as a valid political notion, or that homosexuality is a curable disease as a scientific theory, or that women are less skilled in abstract thinking as a biological fact, these ideas must not be excluded because of *who* presents them. On the face of it, this looks like a contradiction, or a double standard. But the point is that some ideas can be and indeed routinely are excluded from debate, but nobody must be excluded from participating in the debate based on personal traits. The difference is that one set of exclusive criteria screens out obsolete ideas so that everyone can get on with the project of advancing the truth, while the other set of inclusive criteria ensures that everyone can participate in the debate on equal terms.

THE UNIVERSITY'S COMMITMENT TO EQUAL PARTICIPATION

All universities apply criteria to admit students and appoint the faculty. But once students have been admitted and faculty appointed, according to a complex screening process centered on professionally agreed-upon qualifications, none among them must be excluded from participating in the open exchange of ideas based on non-academic criteria. These include the essential characteristics of a person. When critics and watchdog groups describe the university as lacking "viewpoint diversity" and fault colleges for not indiscriminately including all ideas for debate, they conflate these two sets of criteria. They believe that academic freedom in a university means that anyone may say anything, when in fact the university depends on professionally agreed-upon mechanisms in order to advance knowledge in the form of scholarly consensus. The university also has rules of conduct, and a direct legal requirement, that prohibit discriminating against individuals based on group belonging. These ground rules, along with the modicum of decency required for an academic community as it is for any social group, do not prohibit but make viewpoint diversity a reality. The open exchange of ideas in the academic context means that everyone has the equal right to participate once they have been admitted. Put philosophically: the notion of free speech is meaningless, or, in Hannah Arendt's words, "a farce," unless each individual's right to free speech is guaranteed equally.

The principle of equal participation is as important for the university's functioning as the reliance on expertise. But equality in the university setting is not only a pedagogical tool aimed to allow the widest range of potentially useful contributions. It is also a legal mandate. Universities are prohibited, by federal legislation under the congressional act of Title VI and Title IX, from discriminating against, or directly or indirectly excluding students based on essential characteristics. A college with federal funding must not restrict upper-level physics courses to male students, limit membership in the debate team to Christian students, or keep foreign-born students out of the University Senate. There can be separate teams and clubs, but all students must be provided with access to equivalent venues and organizations. All parts of the university, including all of its programs and activities, must be open on an equal basis to all enrolled and qualified students. This equality principle, it turns out, is also a fundamental condition of free speech.

FREE SPEECH IS GROUNDED IN EQUALITY

This all seems like a complicated but still manageable problem. Universities must regulate speech to serve teaching and research, with a light touch and deep expertise; they must also ensure that everyone can participate in debate on equal terms. In virtually all of the campus debates, however, America's sacred right to free speech collides with the third rail of American politics and culture, namely race. This is a crucial point. Many commentators prefer to turn the debate into a high-minded one over abstract conceptions of personal liberty and legal precedents, without wishing to engage with the specific content of actual speech. They do not want to contend with the ideas of virulent racists and white supremacists, who use the university for publicity, have no interest in debate, and advance an agenda that denies our history's legacy of racism. They present a conflict between the liberty of various individuals pitted against other values in a neutral space, where power and history play no part. But "speech" as a concept only has meaning within specific contexts where people are situated differently. In virtually all conflicts over speech on campus, the value of free expression, rightly considered the engine of our democracy, touches upon the principle of equality, anchored in our nation's foundational idea that "we hold these truths to be self-evident, that all men are created equal."

The university context is actually a very useful setting for understanding that without equality, enshrined in our *Declaration of Independence* of 1776 as a non-negotiable premise and formally added to the Constitution, with the ratification of the Fourteenth Amendment, it makes little sense to insist on free expression as a fundamental right. We can recognize, as Hannah Arendt reminds us in a commentary on Thomas Jefferson, that "equality, if it is to be politically relevant, is a matter of opinion, and not 'the truth.'" This means for our purposes here, that unquestioningly upholding equality, even if you consider it one opinion among others, is the voluntary price for admission into university debates. Equality, Jefferson recognized, is "in need of agreement and consent," and yet he posited it as the non-negotiable premise with which we *have to* agree and to which we *must* consent, as true Americans. Unless everyone can participate in speech on equal terms and without a priori exclusions, the freedom to speak one's mind will not result in the desired outcome, which is the robust vetting all of possible ideas.

As it does in other areas of our culture, the confluence of individual rights and fundamental equality makes it harder, rather than easier, to disentangle the issues. We should see free speech and equality not in opposition, not on a collision course that needs to be sorted out by the courts, but as inextricably linked in the functioning of the university. Once we recognize this interdependence of academic freedom and equality in the university, of free and even contentious debate with participation on equal terms, it becomes possible to disentangle the vexing issues found in campus conflicts.

THE BRIGHT LINE ON SPEECH

Indeed, based on these considerations, I propose to draw a bright yet very narrow line around a specific type of speech that undermines the equal participation in the university. There are some ideas that are not only obsolete, not only settled long ago, but also undermine the university's functioning. Let us return to the example of white supremacist speakers, some wearing khakis and polo shirts, and others wielding guns and torches, who claim that some racial groups are inherently inferior. Of course people are different. But the notion that some groups are innately inferior, rather than just different; that there are inferior races; that women are inherently less capable than men, and that this alleged inferiority translates into and justifies political inequality; is not worth discussing in a university. Indeed, eliminating such notions from university debate will not significantly skew public discourse, where racism continues to flourish.

To arrive at this very narrow exclusion of ideas that do not merit debate and do not deserve the status of tax-supported platforms, I offer five reasons. First, such ideas make a mockery of the concept of free speech by severing it from equality, which endows the principle of free expression with meaning and force. Second, ideas of a particular group's innate inferiority, whether this takes the form of white supremacy, or virulent anti-Muslim or anti-Semitism, unacceptably alter the conditions for speech on campus by requiring some students, faculty, or members of the staff to prove their humanity as a condition of participation, while others can confidently take their humanity for granted. Third, ideas of some humans' innate inferiority have been disproven by expert consensus. Fourth, such ideas of innate inferiority lead to behavior that is illegal and unconstitutional in our country, and specifically so in a university, which is bound by federal law to uphold equal conditions of participation. Fifth, the idea that some people are not fully human and therefore do not deserve the protections afforded to human life serves as a direct incitement to violence. Proof of that fact lies in all of recorded history.

The university has an obligation to provide security during an event. But this does not only mean posting security officers, or waiting until a student is physically attacked. It also includes protecting students who would easily be singled out for attack, because they belong to a minority group, as a result of speech that designates them not as different but as inherently inferior.

For speakers who advance the idea of racial and other inherent superiority of some groups, I argue that the idea of organizing society around the supremacy of the "white race," or subordinating women to secondary status, does not merit debate on campus. To debate the idea of racial superiority does not serve the university's fundamental mission, or what the law calls its "compelling interest," since it re-hashes a disproven theory which had once been popular but, based on expert consensus, is now no different from other obsolete ideas of junk science. In the context of higher education, such speech undermines the conditions for and legal requirement of equal participation on which a university is based, and which has some analogous features to workplace guarantees of equal treatment. By positing that some human beings are inherently inferior to others, white supremacists and virulent racists materially undermine the equal conditions of participation for certain students.

PROVING ONE'S HUMANITY IS NOT REQUIRED IN THE UNIVERSITY

Let's consider a concrete situation. While anyone may debate with a white supremacist, the students, faculty, and staff members in the auditorium, whom the speaker singles out as racially inferior, now have the additional task of proving their equal standing while others remain free, as anyone in the university ought to be, to argue about an idea. The idea of innate racial inferiority transforms the ground rules of the educational space. The requirement to prove one's right to be there interferes with the university's purpose and legal obligation of allowing all qualified individuals to participate on equal terms. It severs the critical link of equality to freedom of speech, which is a key ingredient of education, and also democracy, by allowing anyone to join the debate on terms not restricted by group belonging. Of course, anyone is free to reject these terms. But some students are now enjoined to justify their participation in the debate not based on what they know but on who they are. This is not idle speculation. If you have recently visited an American college campus, save for the important HBCU's, or historically Black colleges and universities, you know that especially in elite institutions and flagship campuses, minority students do not make up a significant part of the student population. You also know that in our pluralistic and diverse universities, many students' ethnicities—white, Black, Hispanic, Asian, Pacific-Islander, or any of the categories not yet captured by either law or culture—can be identified visually. When someone argues that specific racial groups are inherently inferior, students belonging to such groups are not only put on the defensive by these "fighting words," which is incidentally a category of speech the Supreme Court does not recognize as protected. The educational setting has been undermined. When a visitor to the physics department argues that women are by nature not equipped for high-level science, it changes the educational space in unacceptable ways. Female students, faculty, and staff, which still make up only a fraction of

endorsed an abstract notion of absolute speech for its own sake. Rather, Douglass explained and embodied the inextricable link between equality and freedom of speech in ways that deepen rather than trouble our commitment to free speech.

Here are Douglass's words, which could be spoken by any of today's students in attendance at a white supremacist's campus visit:

> Would you have me argue that man is entitled to liberty? that he is the rightful owner of his own body? . . . To do so, would be to make myself ridiculous, and to offer insult to your understanding.

For Douglass, the need to prove his humanity is not an acceptable premise. Douglass demonstrated that the requirement for Black Americans to prove their humanity eviscerated our nation's fundamental commitment to equality. Ultimately, and after so many Americans paid the ultimate price over this issue during the Civil War, the Supreme Court and Congress issued rulings and legislation that agreed with Douglass. They did so because this requirement to argue for one's liberty undermined the very premise of free speech, since the freedom for everyone to express his or her opinion also required equal rights to participate in speech. If some people are expected to prove their humanity, as a prerequisite for participating in civic life, the defense of absolute speech rights in public life and in the university in particular becomes a meaningless abstraction. In the university, it becomes an instrument to undermine education's key ingredient of equality of participation.

Douglass, whose significance matches that of the Founders, showed that speech without equality deprives the principle of freedom of speech of its power and significance. When the neo-Nazis and the Klan invoke an absolute right to speak on campus, they undermine the link between equal participation and freedom of expression that is central to education. Importantly, their appeal to absolute speech rights on a college campus also undermines a condition of modern democracy, which is the participation of equals. But the connection of speech to equality is not incidental, or arbitrary. Without allowing all of its members to participate, the university's promise of reasoned argument and constructive disagreement is hollow at best. Without equality, which universities are legally required to uphold, the freedom of speech that allows, in principle, for the robust vetting of many viewpoints has no traction. Equality here means not a bland sameness, but the equality of opportunity, which in the university is the equal right to participate in the often collaborative but sometimes also fiercely competitive exercise of learning through reasoned debate. Equality here means the right to compete on one's merits and not to be excluded based on other factors based on one's personhood.

The point is not about students feeling safe, welcome, and not offended, but it is a matter of all students, regardless of their group belonging, having the equal right to participate. A white supremacist's speech might upset people, excite some, incite others, or offend them. In the public sphere, anyone may choose to attend such an event and either celebrate or protest the speaker's presence. But the controversies about speech on campus—and this is crucial —are about equality of participation as a critical factor of education deserving of that name, and not about offense.

THE EXPERIENCE OF
BEING SILENCED

My instinct is to allow as much speech as possible in college. I am a naturalized American citizen and fiercely proud of rights that other Americans occasionally seem to take for granted. Like many others who had the unparalleled privilege of attending college in the United States, I have been fortunate to benefit, not only as a student but throughout my career as a teacher for over twenty-four years and also as a former senior administrator for over a decade, from robust, contentious, and difficult debates in some of the greatest educational institutions in the world. I have conducted over 50 in-depth conversations with leading scholars and with a diverse group of students who have either written about or found themselves in the midst of speech controversies. I also learned that sometimes we must listen, without responding right away, to people who voice a grievance, and that such listening does not mean surrendering the principle of open debate. Until an exchange year in high school near Philadelphia, after which I moved to the United States and attended the University of California at Berkeley as a freshman, I had been raised in then West Germany, a vibrant democracy that regulates speech differently than the United States. It has placed limitations on hate speech, specifically racially incendiary speech, to prevent a resurgence of the violent and ultimately genocidal racism that culminated in the Holocaust. But aside from once living in a place where the careful and judicious regulation of speech serves to *protect* democracy, in academic settings and also at family gatherings in my adopted country of the United States I have had the uncomfortable experience of others expecting me to remain silent, when they talked about and to me, because my ancestors belong to a nation which committed unforgivable crimes. When I first arrived in this country as a teenager, I didn't know how to respond to such experiences. A Jewish student in my suburban school walked out of a history class when I was asked to talk about Germany. A neighbor showed me the number tattooed on her arm and asked what my grandparents had done during the war. People casually joked that I must be a "Nazi," since I grew up in Germany. These scenes have left me hurt, unsettled, and at a loss. But I sensed that it was not only not my place to speak about and defend myself or explain things. It was not my place to speak, although I was expected to be silent because of things *I* had not done, and for which *I* was not responsible. It was the group I belonged to, and the crimes Germans had committed long before I had been born. I learned that sometimes it is important to suppress the instinct to speak out, which we all experience as urgently and viscerally as the need for air, in order to let others talk about their experiences.

When the neighbors of my host family, who had hired me to help out in their yard, showed me the numbers tattooed on their arms during the Holocaust, I intuited that their experience required me to be silent rather than defensive, to opt for listening carefully instead of hastily explaining that I had been born over two decades after the end of World War II. What should I say: That I did not do this? That nobody in my family was directly responsible? During dinner, I felt responsible for suffering I could not comprehend and had not caused. I learned later that grievances are sometimes directed at me, as a white man and as a university administrator, even though personally I may hold no direct responsibility for an injustice. I was naturalized as an American citizen as an adult. I speak with an accent, and am often identified, without prompting, as not a native-born American. And yet

I have felt the need, at the same time, to acknowledge my complicity in, and the benefit I derive from, whiteness—even though I arrived in this country as an adult—and what that means in this country regardless of my actions. As a white person in America, one may be blamed for the legacy of slavery, for segregation, and for today's racism, regardless of one's personal history, or actions and attitude. As a man, one may be blamed for legal and cultural forms of gender inequality, regardless of one's actions or beliefs. I had to think about such accusations, as a foreign-born American man, to grasp their implication. I learned that these statements are not always personal attacks, although they can be, and that they do not have to be met with defensiveness.

These grievances, often voiced in today's university and also the public debate with great passion, hark back to injustices that we thought we had overcome as a nation, but which continue to shape our shared present. They require everyone to acknowledge that their role in a society still plagued by racism and sexism is not determined only by their own convictions, actions, and choices, or that they are exempt from the historical and social reality others have experienced very differently. It is possible to act in ways that counter the unjust effects of such a world, for example by employing a subtler and nuanced notion of speech rights in situations where moral leadership calls for the condemnation of virulent views.

CONTROVERSIAL SPEECH, ATTENTIVE SILENCE

As a parent, a teacher, and an American, I strive to listen to what the younger generation says. I have found it more productive, even during student protests and angry confrontations, to assume, rather than defensive indignation, a stance of a momentary "attentive silence." I borrow this concept and practice from 20th-century French philosopher Simone Weil. Weil developed this notion of a suitable attitude for anyone charged with administrating, governing, or guiding others, in a 1940s' proposal for reconstituting French democracy after the tyranny of Nazi occupation. She suggested balancing one's personal authority, institutional power, and experience, when in a leadership position, with deliberate attentiveness, rather than a rush to judgment, when listening to those with fewer opportunities for presenting their views. A similar stance of careful listening had been advocated some 2,000 years earlier by Roman emperor Marcus Aurelius, under very different conditions, as a way of guarding leaders against falsely assuming they fully understand those they govern. "A lot of things," Aurelius advises in a reference to seemingly unreasonable complaints, "are means to another end." Aurelius meant that leaders ought to listen beyond the noise, beyond the ad-hominem attacks and anger, beyond the impassioned accusations, to discern that perhaps they are only the addressees of a yet-unclear complaint, and to identify the actual problem by careful listening.

From the experience of teaching and writing about literature and poetry, I have learned to listen closely when someone is trying to express something even when the right vocabulary, the proper legal phrase, or the best political strategy has not yet been found. Literature in particular has taught me to listen to the expression of various forms of life before they are categorized, addressed, and regulated by rules and laws. It taught me to listen attentively to both sides when a person becomes upset or suddenly falls silent once another person says something the speaker may consider innocuous or merely coarse. Through this habit of listening closely to both sides, of recognizing that the impact on a listener is not always linked to a speaker's intention, I noticed, as I explain below, how progressives and conservatives defend very different things when they cite the same absolute principle of free speech. I am not mainly concerned with instances of hypocrisy, in moments when speech rights are used to defend a racist rally but athletes are denounced for taking a knee during the national anthem. Rather, I look at the underlying assumptions of self-styled speech absolutists of all political stripes who join forces to defend extremist speakers but for very different reasons.

I noticed how people miss the significance of speech on campus because they frame the issue as an abstract legal matter without considering the university's specific purpose, which is based on a culture of equality and expertise and on the crucial distinction between academic freedom and freedom of speech. I saw the circularity of arguing that free speech is a uniquely American value because it is a constitutional amendment, and it is a constitutional amendment because free speech is uniquely American. I saw an urgent need to explain how universities, ruled by both formal policies and unwritten norms, differ from other workplaces and the public at large. I was frequently warned about the slippery slope produced by any speech regulation. But there is no evidence, and I consider it highly unlikely, that excluding the claim that some groups are inherently inferior from the university will open the floodgates to governmental speech suppression. What is true, generally speaking, is that Americans believe that regulating speech leads to tyranny, while the citizens of other democratic nations believe that *not* regulating speech leads to tyranny. I recognize and deeply sympathize with the knee-jerk defense of free speech as a defense of democratic rights and norms of behavior that seem under threat in many places in the world currently, including in the United States. I also found a need to wrest back terms that have been hijacked and emptied of meaningful content, of which the notion of "free speech" is a prime example, and to deprive the term "snowflake," meant to disparage students to whom Marcus Aurelius and Simone Weil would surely have listened, of its sarcasm and sting.

I have listened. Now it is time to speak up. The evening after I published an opinion piece in the *New York Times,* reprinted in this book as chapter 4, my inbox was flooded with passionate responses. My teenage children checked online. "You're kind of a mini-celebrity," my son said. "You should accept all invitations to go on live TV." I explained why I first wanted to listen to the responses to my argument and develop it further, which would not happen easily on social media or in the give-and-take of a news program. Reacting to the more colorful and graphic responses to my editorial, my daughter expressed concern. I explained why the topic of free speech, where personal experience and political beliefs intersect in the deeply visceral, immediate need to express ourselves, always elicits heated debate. After a few moments' reflection, she said: "If you really believe what you said, then you have to say it again."

I am heeding her advice. I argue for a definition of free speech that does not undercut the equality necessary for speech to be meaningful in the university. I draw a sharp distinction between free speech in the name of freedom and an atrophied or even weaponized conception meant to stifle the next generation's courageous expansion of equality and freedom for ever more Americans. The speech conversation is about equality, not about offense. In this book I speak for myself, and not for any institution, to reframe a debate that too often shuts down the urgent conversations about our individual and collective commitment to freedom, truth, and equality, which are vital not only for the university but for democracy at large.

2

FROM SKOKIE

TO CHARLOTTESVILLE

Tolerating versus Condoning Speech

IN 1977, THE ACLU DEFENDED on free speech grounds a planned march by neo-Nazis through the village of Skokie, Illinois, the home of many Holocaust survivors. The town had sought to stop the march based on a local ordinance regulating inflammatory speech. In federal court, the neo-Nazis won the right to march, carrying swastika flags and shouting anti-Semitic chants, which they eventually did without much incident in another township in nearby Chicago. In spite of the small number of participants, the march gained national prominence as a test case for our country's enduring commitment to free speech. When the ACLU decided to take the neo-Nazis' case to defend their speech, explicitly without consideration of the message or its impact on the people in the town, some 35,000 members left the ACLU in protest. Nobody was injured or killed during the march, and today the ACLU, alongside scholars and journalists, frequently cites and celebrates the neo-Nazis' court victory against the Village of Skokie as proof of a non-partisan defense of the First Amendment against the impulse to repress and punish offensive or injurious speech. It serves as a case study for law students and is a frequent reference for free speech absolutists. A slew of books and documentaries parse its legal implications.

What would today's America look like if the neo-Nazis had lost their case? According to the ACLU, if the march had been prohibited, our nation would have instantly taken a step on a slippery slope to tyranny. If the neo-Nazis had not marched that day, supporters of the ACLU's actions declare, without a trace of irony, Americans would likely live under conditions close to fascism today. The neo-Nazis' victory and other defenses of hate speech, commentators maintain, safeguarded our democracy. If we are to believe those who criticized the decision, America would have continued to function as a democracy, though with fewer instances of emboldened neo-Nazis and other virulent racists marching under the First Amendment banner.

THE DIFFERENCE BETWEEN TOLERATING AND CONDONING SPEECH

The crux of the argument made by the decision's thoughtful defenders is that virulent anti-Semitism, as objectionable as it may be, poses no significant threat to our democratic life. Lee Bollinger's 1986 landmark study of the Skokie case puts it succinctly: "While anti-Semitism is a problem in American society (just how serious would have been a potential issue in this case), it is not of such magnitude, or so pervasive, as to transform toleration into an act of condonation." If you ask individuals targeted by anti-Semitic and racist attacks, including the family and friends of those murdered by self-declared white supremacists, they might offer another perspective. But legal theorists and philosophers decide on the basis of principles, not personal experience. They seek to weigh a greater good. While they recognize that allowing virulent hate speech creates risks for some members of society, they place the general public's overall commitment to liberty above personal injury, as long as the threat is not immediate, which is rare and then considered a matter of "fighting words." Although the concerns of minority groups are understandable, we are told, they are rooted in the emotions of fear and offense. Since they are not based on reason, they cannot dictate legal outcomes or public life.

But in order to put the abstract principle of speech above any individual's concerns, the defenders of the Skokie decision make a tacit assumption. When they state that the public must tolerate anti-democratic and anti-egalitarian speech, which attacks freedom, justice, and equality, at any cost, they insist in the same breath on our nation's non-negotiable commitment to freedom, justice, and equality. In fact, their defense of speech rights for the enemies of our democracy, they insist, is the strongest expression of this commitment. The ideals of freedom, justice, and liberty, which are our nation's bedrock principles in whose name the pundits, legal scholars, and the ACLU then speak, trump any fringe group's destructive ideas.

When the ACLU defended the neo-Nazis' rights to march, the organization stressed its commitment to democratic ideals. This means that they had to say two things at once. They defended the Nazis' right to speak, to the point of providing them with free legal counsel, but also assured the public that they disagreed with everything the Nazis said. To explain this way of saying two seemingly contradictory things at once, pundits often invoke a sentence attributed, by a later writer, to the 17th-century French philosopher Voltaire: "I disapprove of what you say, but will defend to the death your right to say it."

SUPPORTING SPEECH RIGHTS, NOT THE SPEECH

In order to defend even the vilest speaker's rights, many people make this crystal-clear, quasi-Voltairean distinction between defending someone's speech rights and condemning the specific things they say. In defending the rights for speech they abhor, the neo-Nazis' defenders look philosophically rigorous. They have placed reason above emotion. By relying on an abstract principle and not on fear, offense, or disagreement, and by banking on greater tolerance, they are morally pure.

When the Skokie case caught the public's attention, President Jimmy Carter was asked about it. The country was riled up and unsure; the conflict between the neo-Nazis' rights and the well-being of Skokie's Jewish citizens, including Holocaust survivors, seemed intractable. Carter's response was a textbook example of protecting the right to speak while absolutely condemning the speakers' ideas:

> I deplore it. I wish that this demonstration of an abhorrent po-
> litical and social philosophy would not be present at all . . . .
> We have the same problem, as you know, in other parts of the

Nation—in the South with the Ku Klux Klan, and others . . . .
I think it's best to leave it in the hands of the court.

The president's unequivocal condemnation of Nazi ideas
was critical. By drawing the sharpest possible line between
American values and racist and white supremacist ideas, he
allowed the strongest defense of speech rights not to look like
a tacit condoning of anti-democratic ideas.

Today, something has changed. The new conditions are
not only that white supremacists invade college campuses
in states with open-carry laws, that people have died in
speech conflicts, and that white supremacists have murdered
Americans with shocking regularity. Today's universities also
enroll more diverse students. In 1976, American colleges
and universities had enrolled 84% white students of a total
of about 11 million students, of which 53% were men. By
2014, this number has changed to 58% white students of a
total of 21 million students, with 57% women of all enrolled
students. Today's universities have yet to catch up to this reality by overhauling antiquated norms and implementing
new policies that guarantee equal conditions. The students
who do not believe in hosting white supremacists on campus
exhort these institutions to do so. White supremacists, who
lament this demographic shift rather than recognize it as the
realization of the American dream, routinely sue universities
for the right to speak. They cite Skokie as precedent, even
though that case concerned a march in a public space. But
what has changed on a deeper level, and which we have yet
to fully grasp, is that President Trump is the first president
in modern memory not to unequivocally condemn the neo-
Nazis and the Klan. In his failure to distance himself strongly
from virulent racists and then leave the matter entirely to

the courts, President Trump differs from every president, regardless of party affiliation, from Jimmy Carter's remarks on
Skokie forward.

We might view a president's remarks, such as the
statements offered by Carter, Ronald Reagan, George H. W.
Bush, Bill Clinton, George W. Bush, and Barack Obama
about the abhorrence of virulent racism, to be little more
than symbolic platitudes. All speech issues are a legal matter
to be decided in the courts, as Carter himself declared, and
not a political issue to be adjudicated by the president. While
we may wish for moral leadership, we can rely on our laws,
and proceed without presidential guidance when it may be
lacking.

What has changed, however, is that the bright line between tolerating a speaker's rights and condoning his views,
which is the principle behind the law, is no longer as clear as
it needs to be. The critical distinction between tolerating and
condoning hateful speech was put to the test in 2007 when
as president of Columbia University, Lee Bollinger hosted
then Iranian president Mahmoud Ahmadinejad. While
introducing his invited guest, Bollinger criticized the speaker.
The balancing act of tolerating but not condoning and even
explicitly condemning the speech tested the conventions of
hospitality. In his speech, President Ahmadinejad censured
Bollinger for disparaging him, for not allowing the student
audience to make up their own minds, and for not upholding
the rules of open debate. The question is not to decide
who was right. The point is to highlight the role of power
when it comes to the distinction between tolerating versus
condoning speech: the power to host a debate, the power to
set and enforce its rules, the power to address the audience,
and the power of running an institution such as a university

or a country. The point is also to stress that the university is the site where political and institutional power is checked by more than power, namely by the language of argument rather than the language of emotion or force, and by respect for the truth.

President Ahmadinejad considered it a breach of protocol for his host to criticize his views. For him, in an overly rigid interpretation of a point that Bollinger had made in his extensive and well-reasoned argument in favor of tolerating offensive speech, the host's function is to tolerate the speaker's right to speak but to refrain from condoning or condemning him so that the audience can make up their minds freely. But not unlike other controversial speakers, the Iranian president sought out the university to gain legitimacy for his speech in a space where not power but reason and expertise allows us to differentiate among truth, deliberate falsehood, and opinion. In a sense, the politician played a trick on the hosting institution. It's a trick that university administrators do not always acknowledge but which the political theorist Judith Shklar identified long ago: Ahmadinejad politicized the rules of the game, which are the conditions for political views to be expressed. When members of the alt-right descend upon a campus, university leaders are put in a similar position. They have to reassure students, faculty, and staff that allowing and paying for a white supremacist's visit signals their faith in an abstract right to speech that exists outside of politics, but that they strongly condemn his views.

Once President Trump, in his effort to demolish what he viewed as politically correct pieties, equivocated on condemning the white supremacists and identified "very fine people" among a murderous hate group, all other assurances, by university presidents, lawyers, and commentators, sounded different. As long as the nation's highest office had condemned virulent racism as incompatible with our nation, as represented by our elected government's commitment to equality, these notions could be tolerated precisely as just "ideas," which will never be permitted to take root. The courts will defend the Nazis' right to express their ideas but the same courts, and the government, will do everything to prohibit these ideas of institutionalized segregation, of differential treatment, and of inequality before the law, from becoming policy or social reality.

Once the forceful official condemnation of the neo-Nazis' views (but not a restriction of their right to speak) has gone missing, the line between reluctantly tolerating and tacitly condoning hateful ideas becomes blurred. Even though the public sphere is largely unregulated, the President's remarks, thanks to the power of his office, broadened the scope of what may be reasonably discussed in public. Virulent racism, and formal segregation, had remained until then beyond the pale of being considered as viable policy. By leaving things momentarily unclear, the remarks introduced the possibility that the executive branch might condone the ideas of some of these speakers, and not just tolerate their right to speak.

THE QUESTION OF SPEECH IS LINKED TO POWER

The point is that the question of free speech is inseparable from the question of power. When the nation's most powerful office does not make a crystal-clear distinction between tolerating and condoning speech that defines minorities as unwanted and undeserving of lawful equality in our country, such an absence of clear condemnation is problematic because the president has actual power. If a regular citizen, a lower-ranking official, or a political candidate made similar claims, which people often do, such statements can be countered, refuted, or debated by others in similar positions, and thus on equal terms. Others can take action, as has happened when politicians and public figures have expressed white supremacist views. When a person with great institutional or political power, and especially a person who can shape the terms of public debate and implement policies, creates the impression that he is defending not an abstract speech right but tacitly endorsing a point of view, this shifts the dynamic. The assurance that hateful fringe groups are entitled to speak but that their speech constitutes no threat to civic life, the safety of which is guaranteed by our government for all people, is no longer a simple and bright line.

The case of Skokie concerned a town, where a group of neo-Nazis claimed their constitutional right to march down a public street. Today, neo-Nazis take aim at the university, where additional and distinct rules apply, even in public institutions that operate as extensions of the government. These rules include everyone's right to participate on equal terms, to ensure the equality of opportunity, the obligation to protect everyone from harm, and the principle that unfettered debate occurs for the purpose of advancing and instilling in students the value of respecting the truth. When virulent racists arrive on campus, waving the First Amendment banner, sporting ACLU pins alongside swastikas, and swearing under oath that they will do everything to prevent violence, do they follow these rules?

When the university provides such speakers with a platform, can students be sure that the administration, which also sets policies about admissions, allocates resources, and is charged with allowing for everyone's equal participation, draws a hard line between supporting a speaker's right to speak and condemning the views that undermine the university's enterprise? The political philosopher Corey Brettschneider has proposed that toleration of hate speech must be paired with strong institutional declarations of opposing values; his idea is that institutions, including universities, can forcefully "speak" through actions against some speakers while supporting their right to speak. But when our nation's leader does not unequivocally distinguish between the government's position and such ideas, how can we be sure that the First Amendment will not undo other constitutional guarantees, and does not become, in the 1949 words of Supreme Court Justice Jackson, who cautioned against rigidly enforcing principles that undermine our democracy, "a suicide pact"?

IS VIOLENCE THE ONLY LIMIT ON SPEECH?

The price for our liberties, free speech absolutists maintain, is the discomfort we experience when encountering vile ideas. The risk that those ideas could engulf our rights at some point is worth taking. In the case of Skokie, the ACLU had defended a hate group's rights not in order to advance the cause of fascism but in order to uphold our nation's democratic values. The risk had been worth it, many commentators maintain, since nobody was injured or killed, and because the neo-Nazis did not carry the day. Charlottesville, where the ACLU again provided the neo-Nazis with free counsel, presents an opportune moment to clarify whether deadly violence is the only place to draw a line. This is the case not only because several people died and more were injured in Charlottesville, but because the neo-Nazis held one of their two rallies on university grounds. They did not want to debate ideas but to claim the space of academia to legitimate their agenda. Their goal was not to persuade others with arguments but to threaten them with force.

In the university, where speech serves a specific rather than general purpose, the line must be drawn to regulate speech that advances learning and research, and speech that materially undermines the equal participation of students in the quest for knowledge. In the university, the right to equal participation cannot be taken for granted. It became a legal requirement, first with Title VI in 1965 and then with Title IX in 1972. But aside from legal protection, speech serves a specific purpose in the university's mission. It carries more weight, rather than less, than on a street corner.

Today, fewer students are willing to view virulent racism and white supremacy as mere ideas that do not materially impact them. They are less willing to shrug off a torch-wielding, weapons-bearing group of men and women in the name of constitutional principles that ought to be invoked in the name of justice and equality, and not division and hatred, by our nation's leaders. They are less trusting that university leaders who defend these principles and also uphold the university's other values, and question whether the defense of abstract speech rights does not contain a sliver of agreement with these points of view.

Nojan Rostami, a senior at the University of Virginia in 2017, explained the struggle to maintain trust in moral leadership: "Instead of saying that the university is going to

keep me and my peers of color safe—or reassuring students
that we belong on our campus and no one can take that from
us—Teresa Sullivan, the president of University of Virginia,
sent out a statement that reminded us that the college 'is a
public institution and follows state and federal law regarding
the public's right to access open spaces.' She wrote that the
University of Virginia supports First Amendment rights
but rejects 'the ideology of intolerance and hate.' [. . .] I'm
trying to be sympathetic [. . .] but it's hard to do that when
I'm staying up on Saturday night fending off nightmares of
armed militiamen dragging me out of my dorm room [. . .]
Those men beat and pepper-sprayed my friends and killed
a young woman in the town I have come to call home." The
University of Virginia has committed enormous resources to
restore the students' faith in their institution. But the back-
drop of this diminished trust in moral leadership, prompted
by a reasonable fear of targeted violence, is captured by *The
Daily Stormer*, a neo-Nazi publication, which characterized
President Trump's post-Charlottesville press appearance as
the refusal to draw a sharp line between upholding a group's
speech rights and condemning their views: "When asked to
condemn, he just walked out of the room. Really, really good.
God bless him."

Many students do not believe that a roving and armed
hate group chanting incitements to violence constitutes no
immediate threat. In preparation for several controversial
speakers, university leaders at different institutions have
encouraged faculty and students to avoid certain locations,
organize counter-events in other locations, or stay off campus
altogether during the time of such events. Such suggestions,
while sensible, draw a line: a line that privileges an external
speaker's right to speak over the right of enrolled students

and faculty to attend their university and participate in all of its offerings on equal terms, and exercise their equal rights. Clearly, the administrators who urge students to stay away recognize there is a problem, and that a line must be drawn somewhere. But why not draw it in a way that includes all students, faculty, and staff regardless of background, instead of drawing a line that asks them to forgo their right to an education? Why draw the line to allow incitement and hate speech, when such speech serves no educational purpose and undermines the very principle of equal participation on which our country's speech rules and the academic enterprise are staked? Why draw it, however inadvertently, by acceding to the alt-right's explicit wishes and urging students and faculty, particularly those of color and other minorities, to stay away from the university on that day? It is this unintended effect of fulfilling the alt-right's wish to return to the era of racial segregation, even if only for a day and in the interest of safety, that challenges the students' trust in their institution's leaders. Why not at least require each speaker to truly engage in a debate with experts, according to the principles of the university community, rather than simply granting them a stage and asking the targets of this vitriol to give up their right to attend school in a non-hostile and physically safe environment? Are speech principles really content-neutral, the students, faculty, and commentators ask, since they know that the university routinely excludes many other ideas based on expert assessment? If the university insists on allowing virulent racists on First Amendment grounds, does it uphold its other commitment to equality via the deployment of resources and binding policies?

The students note that the idea of legally sanctioned inequality, which our country outlawed over a century ago and which had been rooted in junk science, obviously had not been stamped out despite decades of debate, and that sunlight has actually not been the best disinfectant. Even the ACLU has rethought its absolutist position, recognizing that spending resources on people who thumb their noses at the institution's ideals makes people, including donors, uneasy. "Freedom of opinion," Hannah Arendt wrote in a 1967 essay, "is a farce unless factual information is guaranteed and the facts themselves are not in dispute." The students, whether or not they are familiar with Arendt's adage, are not sure that inviting obsolete ideas which dispute established facts back to campus will yield better results this time.

COUNTER SPEECH
WITH MORE SPEECH

After the events in Charlottesville in 2017, faculty, university leaders, and national commentators exhorted the students to counter unreason with reason, and to defeat hatred with tolerance, kindness, and love. Rise above the provocation and bigotry, commentators said. Stage a counter-rally. Trust that the university is committed to your equal participation, even if your administration sponsors a speaker who disputes your right to exist, even if the number of enrolled and graduated minority students has not changed in years, and even if incidents of blatantly unequal treatments are numerous. Others blamed the counter-protesters for the violence that happened. People were heartened by the backlash to the white supremacists in other cities.

But unlike street corners or parks, universities depend on ground rules of mutual respect, on the premise of equal participation, and on the idea that debate serves a purpose. When commentators counseled students to practice forbearance and civility, as did newspaper columnist David Brooks, when he wrote that "the only way to confront fanaticism is with love," they essentially asked them to follow these rules. But in asking students, faculty, and staff to adhere to the ground rules and accommodate people who materially undermine the same ground rules of equal participation, the university applies a double standard. When the issue is one of someone being offended, the university might be able to maintain this tension. In instances when the speaker refuses to adhere to the rules, however, this double standard undoes the university's purpose. It no longer functions as a community of people who share the goal of advancing knowledge and respecting the truth, but becomes an unregulated public space indistinguishable from any street corner.

The students take seriously the self-evident truth that once admitted to the university, as far as group belonging, they have a right to equal participation. They do not accept that they must defend a neo-Nazi's rights to speak who disputes Jewish, Black, and other minority students' right to exist. They also do not accept at face value the hypocrisy of organizations who defend a neo-Nazi's right to speech, ostensibly to uphold his constitutional rights against state suppression, and at the same time submit legislative bills mandating penalties for students who exercise their right to political protest. Such selective and dishonest application of constitutionally guaranteed rights reveals the intent of subjugating others, most often racial minorities and women, under the weaponized idea of free speech.

Charlottesville brought to light deeper problems than how to balance individual speech rights and equality. Our nation's universities have regularly admitted women and minority students for more than half a century but still struggle with providing all students with legally required equal participation. When a speaker disputes the rights of minority students to participate in a university on equal terms, this imposition harks back to a time, which in disturbing instances persists even today, when women and minority students, in every class, every day, at every classroom door and college gate, and even in their own dormitories, had to prove their right to belong. Let them prove it, some may say. Let them become more resilient in college, so they will be ready for the real world. But such an unequal requirement, which is not expected of all students, is prohibited by law. To refer back to the arguments made in the wake of Skokie, today's neo-Nazis and white supremacists should not be barred from a public space, such as a park or street corner. Like their forebears in Skokie, they may march in the streets to promote obsolete and long-settled ideas of racial supremacy. But in a university, they undermine the very premise of education, which depends on the equal participation of all members of the community, regardless of background and race.

Charlottesville, if we choose to pay attention, requires us to be more honest about the difference between absolute speech rights and academic freedom of inquiry. It also creates a challenge for the practice of drawing a bright line between tolerating versus condoning a position which hopes to admit ideas, after appropriate vetting but without adjudicating their merit, for unfettered debate to advance knowledge. Charlottesville encourages us to insist on our constitutional obligation to uphold educational equality, even when the courts wrong-headedly subordinate educational equality in a narrow application of First Amendment orthodoxy. These events also force us to think about how the impact of any given speaker depends not on whether what he says is true, just, or right, but simply on the fact that his speech is issued from a powerful platform. The violence wrought by the white supremacists is no reason to enact draconian speech codes. But a speaker's refusal to accept the basic protocol and rules of university life necessitates a clearer statement on these ground rules, and a refusal to let others manipulate these rules in ways that undermine the university's purpose.

If Skokie was a victory for free speech, did the neo-Nazis' march expose vile ideas of virulent racism to sunlight, where they withered and died? It remains an open question whether the court's robust protection especially of "group defamation" over the past 50 years, which is the legal term for racist expression, has improved race relations and equality in this country. Indeed, much of the debate over speech hinges on this last question, and the students are asking a far more profound question about democracy than their critics like to admit. Has the robust protection of group defamation, ushered in by court decisions in the early 1960s, after the Supreme Court had initially restricted hate speech in the 1950s, when the threat of fascism and anti-Semitism was considered more immediate and real, helped or hindered the cause of equality? This is the question at the heart of today's campus controversies: is our country better off in 2018 because the courts have protected hate speech above other types of speech? Or is the country worse off in 2018 because hate speech and anti-democratic activism have been granted special protection not accorded to other types of speech? Or are the rules in need of revision because the Founders couldn't foresee the capacities of the internet? Are "hate-speech rules [. . .] evidence of a commitment to democratic dialogue," as Richard Delgado and Jean Stefancic maintain, or do such rules suppress democracy, as scholars such as Nadine Strossen, Floyd Abrams, and others argue? The answer to this question is not a litmus test on one's commitment to the Constitution. But it forces us to state whether we consider equality as much a bedrock principle of our democracy as freedom of expression.

According to Strossen, Abrams, Timothy Garton Ash, and others, allowing and indeed especially protecting hate and ignorance exposes such ideas to light and reason, where they will wither and die. Penalizing certain specific forms of such expression, especially US based scholars argue, undermines democracy itself. The idea is that protecting people's right to insult, demean, and degrade strengthens democracy. But has progress truly been helped by hate speech? Or has the persistence of racism harmed the country as a whole? Did white supremacy and racism really suffer a blow when the neo-Nazis were allowed to march in Skokie? In the setting of the university, this question is put into sharp relief. Does the presence (and the administration's explicit protection) of hate speech help or hinder the equal conditions of learning for students? Are deliberate falsehoods and the intentional denial of proven facts conducive to study and research, when they are not presented as part of a pedagogical exercise? How can universities defend hate speech on a principle of content-neutrality that is not applicable to countless other ideas in academia, without making the defense of hate speech *in particular* an attack on the guarantee of equality?

3

FREE SPEECH IS ROOTED

IN EQUALITY

Frederick Douglass and Our Country's Inalienable Rights

I have a quarrel with those who fling the weight of the Constitution against the cause of human liberty.

—FREDERICK DOUGLASS (1857)

AN INCENDIARY SPEECH

In 1854, a speaker was invited to address the graduating class of Western Reserve College, in Hudson, Ohio, known today as Case Western Reserve University. The commencement speaker was a well-known public figure who often expounded on views deemed offensive, incendiary, and even treasonous by a great many Americans. Indeed, the invitation to Frederick Douglass was a deliberate provocation of public sentiment in a nation roiled by the dispute whether Congress, rather than individual states, had jurisdiction over slavery. Even in Congress, governed by procedural rules to ensure robust but reasoned debate, the mere discussion of the abolition of slavery had been prohibited for eight consecutive years, from 1836 to 1844, via a "gag rule."

In 1856, Massachusetts senator Douglas Sumner had been caned nearly to death by a South Carolina Representative for criticizing slavery. Many Southern papers and one of the country's oldest collegiate organizations, the Jefferson Literary and Debating Society at the University of Virginia, had praised the violent attack on a speaker who had raised this incendiary topic. For a great number of Americans, then, Douglass's commencement address was a deeply offensive speech that would incite imminent violence, foment treason, and lead to unlawful behavior.

Given that his topic was so controversial, Douglass's speech would seem to be a forerunner of the type of contemporary speech that needs to be protected at all cost but prompts such outcries, and even violence, on campuses today. When President Trump praised Douglass, albeit without displaying deep knowledge of Douglass's achievements, he joined a chorus of conservative authors and pundits who regularly invoke Douglass exactly in this manner, as a crusader for absolute speech rights, and as one of their own. To be sure, as biographer David Blight points out, Douglass is a malleable figure but in addition to being "a serious constitutional thinker," he was a radical. Far from advocating for abstract principles divorced from context and deliberately blind to content, like some of today's conservatives, Douglass powerfully anticipates the argument that freedom of speech has true force and meaning only when this hallowed American principle is rooted in equality.

Douglass shows how today's self-declared free speech absolutists not only fail to acknowledge our country's changing conception of free speech—they also make a mockery of this essential concept when defending hate speech above all else. In the context of legislative and juridical suppression of a mere discussion of the inherent wrong of slavery, Douglass had hesitated in accepting the invitation out of concern for his personal safety. There was no ACLU to protect him, and he could not call on First Amendment jurisprudence, at a time when the Supreme Court consistently ruled against the equality of Black Americans, and would not cite the First Amendment until 1919, to protect his right to express a point of view which many Americans considered deeply offensive and an incitement to treason. Indeed, as a Black American he had no legal standing to claim a right that the Founding Fathers had considered innate, but only for white men. And yet he spoke. Today, of course, many people, including our president and conservative pundits, will echo a contemporary Northern newspaper's grandiose assertion that Douglass "ascending the platform [was] a triumph for humanity." But before filing his commencement speech as a further step in our nation's inevitable progress toward ever more expansive speech rights, we must note that Douglass spoke without First Amendment protection. His speech underlines the idea that the principle of free speech must be anchored in equality, rather than appealing to an abstract legal definition, to ring true.

SPEAKING OUTSIDE THE LAW

> Would you have me argue that man is entitled to liberty? that he is the rightful owner of his own body? . . . To do so, would be to make myself ridiculous, and to offer insult to your understanding.

Douglass spoke these crucial words on yet another occasion where he asserted his right to speak without a court's or congressional blessing, on July 5, 1852, in Rochester, New York, to celebrate our Republic's 76th anniversary. Douglass here followed in the footsteps of great orators, such as the Greek statesman Demosthenes and the Roman consul Cicero, who spoke to defend freedom. He rousingly presented the religious, moral, social, political, and legal reasons that the legal and social inequality of people based on race and gender contradicts our nation's constitutional principles and fundamental values. When considered from the perspective of speech rights, Douglass points out a glaring contradiction in today's bipartisan defense of absolute rights for speech that undermines our nation's commitment to equality. When eminent scholars but also conservative pundits enlist Douglass as a forerunner of free speech absolutism, they suppress his central argument that speech must be rooted in equality to have any traction. Unless there is equality, the freedom to speak remains reserved for only some people. Speech that suppresses equality, Douglass made clear in ways we have yet to fully realize, cannot be defended on freedom of speech grounds in a meaningful sense. It is important to underline that Douglass, who lived from 1818 to 1895, did not speak under the protection of the First Amendment. The Amendment played an insignificant role in our country's jurisprudence until early in the 20th century. It was never cited during the 19th century by our Supreme Court but first applied in 1925 to overturn state regulation of speech and used for the first time in 1965 to rule an act of Congress unconstitutional (regulating the mailing of political material). In fact, Douglass spoke against prevailing public sentiment of his era, formalized by the Supreme Court's morally reprehensible "Dred Scott" decision of 1858 and shared by a great number of white people, which ruled that Black Americans

countless lesser known Black Americans who acted as rights-bearing citizens long before the Fourteenth Amendment granted them legal standing, as Martha Jones has superbly chronicled in *Birthright Citizens*, he also exposes the absurdity of expecting some people's speech not to be measured on the strength of their argument but on whether they qualify as fully human.

Douglass says that requiring him to present an argument for his liberty, and thus for the inalienable rights that include freedom of speech, would "offer insult to [his audience's] understanding." He means that such an argument would insult his listeners' intelligence as well as their knowledge, since the self-evident fact—of another human's inherent liberty—is not worthy of any thinking person's deliberation and attention. The request to argue for one's own humanity, which meant in Douglass's time arguing that our country's laws applied to him as a Black man, undermines the very conception of free speech. It would make both the speaker and the concept of freedom "ridiculous," Douglass points out, because his words would have to prove his proper condition as a human being, namely his liberty. But such proof is not something one may present in the form of an argument. Liberty, even when it is the topic and argument of Douglass's speech, is also the self-evident, inviolable, and non-negotiable presupposition for all speech intended to be meaningful for others.

DOES FREE SPEECH DEPEND ON ONE'S LEGAL STATUS?

Douglass's rhetorical question, "Would you have me argue that man is entitled to liberty," constitutes a key moment in America's proud history of free speech. The question identifies our common humanity and our innate capacity for freedom as the precondition of all speech, which must not be subjected to debate. Douglass is indeed one of our country's patron saints of free speech not because of a blanket endorsement of absolute speech rights but because by speaking he links the freedom of speech to freedom and equality. He speaks without having the legal, political, or social right to do so, and in this sense is a true American exemplar of courageous action. His speech transforms the nature of speech in America by underlining its inherent link to freedom and equality, which the First Amendment contains at its core but which our country's dominant legal and political culture does not realize until much later. Indeed, the current campus flare-ups over speech rights for speakers who deny the full humanity of some racial groups are proof that we are still struggling to realize that for speech rights to be meaningful, they must be rooted in equality.

At the center of any consideration of free speech must be the idea that speech can be protected only for individuals who have the right to speak. But anyone can speak! You may object. This is precisely the point. Anyone can speak. But if a speaker is not regarded by law and public sentiment as equally human, his or her speech, regardless of content, is the *production* of the event of free speech where free speech does not exist yet in a meaningful sense. So if a person's humanity is in question, some may suggest, just let this person argue for it! If a virulent racist wants to speak on campus today, let the minority students speak up, just as Douglass did. On purely formal terms, this is feasible. But this expectation, in Douglass's memorable words, makes a "mockery" of our nation's most hallowed principles, namely the truths we hold to be self-evident: that all men are created equal.

> To drag a man in fetters into the grand illuminated temple of liberty, and call upon him to join you in joyous anthems, were inhuman mockery and sacrilegious irony. Do you mean, citizens, to mock me, by asking me to speak to-day?

It is a mockery of free speech to expect someone to prove his own worthiness of speaking in a fundamental sense, as a human being. Douglass is concerned not only with the way he may be set up to perform for his largely white audience, who expect him to prove, or fail to prove, that he is entitled to the right to speak as a human of equal standing. "Is it not astonishing," Douglass says, that in spite of the many things Black Americans are tasked with doing, "we are called upon to prove that we are men!" Douglass knows that his speech is judged not primarily on content but whether it qualifies him as fully human. Such a requirement, which determines who qualifies as a participant in speech, is an inherently different criterion from the standards used to judge the content, coherence, and merits of any other speech. It shifts the criteria from content to power, and from the content to the rules for speech. The restriction that for some people, their speech is measured not on content but on the precondition of the speaker's yet-to-be-proven humanity, which the law or the public may deny, turns the idea of freedom of expression without equality into a meaningless abstraction.

HOW RACIST SPEECH UNDERMINES THE POINT OF FREE SPEECH

Far from being a long-past historical anecdote, Douglass's speech draws our attention to a central dilemma in campus speech controversies. For the concept of free speech to be meaningful, the participation of some speakers must not be restricted on the basis of inalienable qualities. You may be refuted in a debate because your arguments are weak, wrong, or badly phrased, but you must not be excluded a priori based on whether or not you count as fully human. To invite a speaker who categorically excludes some human beings from the consideration of rights, which is what some of the most contentious campus debates are about, severs the idea of speech rights from its goal of protecting individual liberty. A campus visitor who argues that some students are inherently inferior, materially undermines the conditions that make speech free.

Is racism this kind of speech? While I focus here on speech that denies the humanity of some groups, the author and Nobel laureate Toni Morrison reminds us that all forms of racism, rooted in ignorance, insecurity, and unreason, undermine the conditions for equal and open exchange central to a university:

> The function, the very serious function of racism is distraction. It keeps you from doing your work. It keeps you explaining, over and over again, your reason for being. Somebody says you have no language and you spent twenty years proving that you do.

Racism, Morrison reminds us, serves to place additional burdens and requirements on some people, but not others. It alters the conditions of participation not incidentally but by design, and in this way materially undermines the workings of an equality-based society. Douglass showed that the request to explain one's "reason for being" keeps a person not only from doing one's work. Such a requirement, whether explicitly stated or expressed in the garb of pseudo-science, undermines the very fabric of our democracy. To cite the First Amendment as the right to challenge others to prove their reason for being becomes a mockery and, in Douglass's words, a "blasphemous irony." Douglass showed, in direct opposition to the prevailing sentiment and legal rulings of his time, that for the right to speech to mean anything, it must not be parceled out only to some, neither by 435 men and women in Congress sworn to serve the nation, nor nine (or six, or eight) black-robed justices, nor one individual sworn to uphold the Constitution in the Oval Office.

THE INHERENT HUMANITY OF ALL IS NOT UP FOR DEBATE

A speaker's full humanity, which I define as one's capacity to imagine a life free from preconceived constraints, ought not to be a matter for debate. At least this should be the case in the 21st century university, where the established fact that all people are fully human has replaced the pseudo-scientific paradigms, some of which were promoted by Thomas Jefferson and persist today, that Douglass helped to overthrow. No student should be compelled to explain his or her being in the university to a speaker who argues that he or she is inherently inferior to others, based on race, gender, ethnicity, or other types of group belonging. If someone wishes to dispute this simple fact and revive some obsolete 19th century pseudo-science, his ideas do not merit debate in a university setting devoted to establishing the truth.

Douglass insisted on this fact. After the Civil War, Congress enshrined this fundamental equality of all human beings, which is the self-evident truth found already in the

Declaration of Independence, in the Fourteenth Amendment of 1868 which extends equal protection under the law, including that of free speech, to all citizens. This basic amendment guaranteeing equality was ratified 16 long years after Douglass gave his speech. Douglass spoke without having the right to speak. It would take several additional decades to secure for women the fundamental right to vote, and nearly a century to pass additional equality laws, starting in the 1960s, that would grant all Americans their personal liberty, rather than reserve liberty only for some. Douglass's speech, and many others by Black people, other minorities, and women, transformed our country's conception of speech by demonstrating that without equality of participation, we forgo our nation's most sacred principle to achieve and protect everyone's freedom.

AMERICA'S STRUGGLE OVER EQUALITY FOR ALL

Douglass identifies the greatest limit to free speech in 1850s America as the fact that those who are barred from speech cannot overcome this suppression of their speech by argument. It is not a matter of inequality, in the sense of individuals having different resources in various contexts. Rather, it is a matter of using completely different and irreconcilable standards: the content of speech for some, their essential humanity for others. If your idea loses out, it's a political defeat. If your identity loses out, you do not exist.

But Douglass ignores this restriction and speaks out. The fact that he speaks amounts to a contradiction. While robustly debating slavery, Douglass disputes the idea that there can be rational, robust, and unfettered debate over the legitimacy of depriving human beings of their freedom. The claim of someone's lesser humanity does not fall under the rubric of free speech. The British philosopher John Stuart Mill, often cited for his passionate defense of personal liberties, including freedom of expression, in his 1859 treatise *On Liberty*, also did not consider the humanity of slaves a matter about which one many have a diversity of viewpoints. "Remember, we consider [slaves] to be human beings, entitled to human rights," Mill wrote in 1862. Mill rejected the Southern states' right to secede in order to keep Black Americans enslaved, as "a strange misapplication of a true principle," since they rebelled by misapplying their right to self-govern (a true principle) to justify their right to suppress another's essential freedom (thus not applying this principle to others). What Mill identifies as a deep contradiction is the same argument used by campus speakers who apply the true principle of speech rights for virulent racists to deprive others of their inherent freedom and of that same right. There can be no mistake here, all abstractions notwithstanding. The Nazis do not visit a campus to fight for the diversity of viewpoints, nor for the principle that the other side deserves a view. They do not want minority students to debate them; they do not want to grant them the same right to speak, or even be present. Their visits have no educational value but materially disrupt the learning environment which all universities, including public ones, are obligated and entitled to design.

In the public at large, such contests over conflicting individual liberties occur frequently, and are regulated by public debate, or our shared laws. In the university, which depends on the equal participation of all constituents in open and robust debate, one person's right to speak must not deprive others of that same right by requiring them to explain their reason for being.

Douglass's argument is broader yet. He renders evident that a genuine marketplace of ideas, which is the public realm, must not include arguments of preemptive exclusion of some groups. This is no different than saying that a free market economy remains free precisely because it allows for the regulation of monopolies, price-fixing, false advertising, etc. A short time after Douglass's commencement address, in 1857, the United States Supreme Court directly contradicted the spirit of the First Amendment so powerfully enacted by Douglass when it ruled that people of African descent cannot be, nor were ever intended to be, citizens under the Constitution. In the specific context of the law, the 1857 *Dred Scott vs. Sandford* decision deprived Black Americans of their legal "standing," which is the right to speak in legal matters on their own behalf, or on behalf of others.

This wrongheaded decision points to a basic tension in the United States. The Founding Fathers guaranteed freedom of expression as an inalienable human right, but non-white Americans and women had to fight for this right via methods neither recognized nor sanctioned by the court. Indeed, the Supreme Court was the institution that deprived more than half of America's citizens of their fundamental freedom for decades. Women in America had to fight until 1920, in struggles with enormous personal sacrifice and against a prevailing notion that women must not speak on their own behalf, to be granted their inalienable right to polit-ical expression by means of the vote. Native Americans were granted full citizenship rights in 1924, but not the full right to vote in all states until 1957, over a century after Douglass used speech to fight for universal suffrage. In a purely legal sense, the country removed this tension when the earlier court decisions were voided and the country recognized the full equality of all Americans. Today, equality is an idea to which all Americans subscribe, if with varying degrees of conviction. Or is equality perhaps not such a pervasive idea, and we should re-examine this principle in a campus debate? To present current speech debates as opening a discussion between individual liberty and equality, where free speech trumps equality, means to revive a long-settled matter in ways that are deeply un-American.

Who Can Draw a Line?

Today, Douglass is frequently cited by pundits as a powerful proponent of absolute freedom of expression. They enlist Douglass's writing and speeches as an example of the maxim that "the remedy to be applied [to defeat bad ideas] is more speech." This notion of countering speech with more speech became something like a mantra of speech absolutists after Supreme Court Justice Louis Brandeis's memorable phrase in a 1925 ruling. But it's not that simple. Douglass considered the expectation to prove his humanity an "inhuman mockery and sacrilegious irony." The requirement to prove his humanity to remedy racial inequality with more speech was not just one more idea in the turbulent and messy marketplace of ideas that is our country's culture. This requirement robbed the notion of freedom of speech of its force. It undermined the idea of the marketplace by barring some speakers from entry. When someone says in public, "you're inherently inferior because of your race," those are fighting words. When someone says those words in the university, where students are instructed not to fight but to defeat speech with more speech, the students thus addressed find themselves in the unacceptable condition of having to prove their humanity.

In his response to the Supreme Court's *Dred Scott* decision, which denied Black Americans the basic rights of all citizens, Douglass equates the abolitionist claim for freedom with free speech itself. The decision remains relevant for any consideration of free speech today, even after the post-Civil War amendments nullified it, since that ruling also, if negatively, linked freedom of speech to freedom itself. Douglass responded to the decision: "Slavery was so weak, and liberty so strong, that free speech could attack the monster to its teeth." Douglass defends free speech not as an abstraction that can be wrapped around any idea but reminds us that this right is in the service of liberty *and* equality, and applies without qualification to all human beings. In his defense of free speech he *excludes* speech, including all of the pro-slavery arguments of his day, that denies the full humanity of others. Douglass pitted free speech against the court's decision, rather than privilege a legal ruling which defined free speech in unequal terms that counter the term's true meaning. Douglass draws a line. And what gives him the right to draw this line that excludes from protection the kind of speech which declares the lesser humanity of some?

When today's conservative pundits cite Douglass as a crown witness upholding free speech in America, people think of the great orator relying on free speech as attacking slavery, as he put it, "to its teeth." But in his argument for abolition, which struck many white Americans as deeply offensive, incendiary, and wrong-headed at the time, Douglass placed the many arguments for slavery, which flourished in politics, science, economics, morality, history, and religion, beyond the pale of ideas worth discussing. When conservative pundits and politicians refer to some humans as inferior, primitives or savages who do not deserve the rights held by other citizens, and then invoke Douglass as a crown witness for promoting free speech, they act in bad faith, or, to use John Stuart Mill's phrasing, they misapply a true principle. When those same pundits arrive at the University of California at Berkeley to cloak themselves in the mantle of the Freedom of Speech Movement, which Mario Savio had initiated in 1964 in the name of racial justice and equality after being a freedom rider in the South, their claims ring hollow. The argument that on today's campuses, students, faculty and staff have to listen to a speaker who promotes the idea that they are inherently inferior, has nothing to do with free speech.

DID FREE SPEECH BRING ABOUT EQUALITY?

Douglass's speech complicates the triumphant story that the First Amendment helped Black Americans, women, and other minorities in their struggle to have their inherent rights, including freedom of expression, recognized. This claim is made often by the ACLU, which had been founded in 1920, when the organization justifies their decision to defend neo-Nazis and the Ku Klux Klan from among the many people who need legal assistance to claim due process, equality, and other rights in our nation. According to David Cole, the ACLU's national legal director, "throughout our history, disadvantaged minority groups have effectively used the First Amendment to speak, associate, and assemble for the purpose of demanding their rights—and the ACLU has defended their right to do so." The constitutional expert Floyd Abrams also insists that the First Amendment has always helped minorities, even though it was not once cited or applied from the date of its ratification in 1791 until 1919. In *The Soul of the First Amendment*, Abrams further explains that the United States protects hate speech since it has no history of racially motivated state-sponsored violence or genocide, unlike democracies such as Germany and South Africa. "It is understandable that some nations have sometimes responded by limiting particularly hateful speech that may have contributed to past tragedies. The United States has been fortunate not to have suffered such horrific events, and I am unwilling to criticize nations that have responded to such calamities by urging them to change their policies. For this nation, though, strict constitutionally imposed limitations on such legislation have served us well." The National Museum of African American History and Culture opened in 2019, after decades-long efforts to highlight the contributions of African-Americans to our society and to commemorate the ravages of slavery. It is located 1.6 miles from the United States Supreme Court. The National Museum of the American Indian is located less than a mile from our highest court. In those places, as in countless schools, libraries, on the internet, and through conversations, anyone can learn to differ with Mr. Abrams on his claim that the United States has suffered no "such horrific events," and refer to the genocide of Native Americans and the enslavement of Africans which lasted from 1619–1865. In 2000, the head of the United States Bureau of Indian Affairs offered a formal apology for the agency's role in the "ethnic cleansing" of indigenous people in the Western United States. The point is not to create false and misleading equivalencies, and Abrams is correct to differentiate between the incommensurate and truly incomparable horrors of the Holocaust, apartheid, and crimes such as chattel slavery and the genocide of Native Americans. But has our varying legislation around hate speech, which Abrams defends by omitting a crucial part of our nation's history, really "served us well"? Differently put, who in America has benefitted from the protection of hate speech, which Abrams unequivocally champions especially for vile and incendiary speech?

Douglass gives the lie to the ahistorical claim that the strong protection of hate speech has been good for all members of our democracy. Most of our country's freedom fighters spoke out either at a time when the First Amendment played an insignificant role in our country's legal and public culture, or when the courts consistently ruled against their very right to speak. They spoke out explicitly *against* a narrow and rigid interpretation of speech rights as applicable only for some Americans, rather than to all as diverse equals. Many of them did not use the First Amendment in any technical or legal sense, but spoke out against a legal and political system that turned this principle against them.

There are two points here. First, in the specific context of the university, where equality is both a legal and pedagogical requirement, such rigid jurisprudence is not useful to define the enabling condition of speech. In the university, Stanley Fish, Carolyn Rouse, Robert Post, Prudence Carter, Sigal Ben-Porath and others have pointed out, speech does not operate as a legal abstraction devoid of content and circumstance. Second, the First Amendment is not a self-enforcing tool that guarantees individual liberty on equal terms for all. Douglass shows that unless freedom of speech is rooted in equality, the concept remains an abstraction robbed of the emancipatory thrust intended by the framers. It is a concept that has been interpreted differently throughout our nation's history, and that has not always protected everyone's freedom on equal terms. We have a constitutional obligation to insist on speech rights for all, and not only for some who want to deprive others of that right. Douglass's speech is so crucial in reminding us that free speech protection is all but meaningless when severed from equality. Many other thinkers have conceptualized equality as well as liberty, including freedom of speech, along these lines. Notably, and despite the fact that their radical critique compels us to rigorously examine what is really at stake rather than offering a complete solution, many of these have encountered severe rejection in addition to important critique, like legal scholar Catharine MacKinnon. Our nation's history demonstrates that speech rights, when severed from equality, do not automatically end up protecting the civil freedom of the powerless.

The true tradition of free speech in America consists of speakers like Douglass who refuse an overly rigid definition of absolute rights, severed from equality and freedom. Such a conception, in direct contradiction to the country's laws which have always recognized limitations on speech, has been wielded as a weapon against disenfranchised groups from the founding days of the Republic, in a series of shameful court decisions, and all the way to recent campus protests, by conservative and liberal self-styled free-speech advocates alike. There are indeed "two very different visions of free speech" at work in our country, as lawyer Floyd Abrams points out in citing Kathleen Sullivan, a former dean of the Stanford Law School. But we do not have to choose between the realities of apolitical equality and personal liberty. There is no evidence to show that regulating speech inevitably leads to tyranny, nor is there a guarantee that the First Amendment, which was ratified in 1791, automatically protects all Americans' rights. It is not a self-enforcing law but a principle that needs to be applied in the awareness that free speech is meaningless when it is granted only to some, and used to deprive others of that right. In Douglass's time, limiting the speech of minorities protected the rights of white Americans. By stressing the link of equality and freedom, rather than setting these rights in opposition, our country can prevent compromising the rights of minorities in order to protect the rights of those in power.

We ought to guard against the overly rigid conception of the First Amendment, which had not stopped the systematic disenfranchisement of non-white Americans and women for longer than a century, and instead encourage a vivid conception of free speech that grants these rights to *all*. We do not need to fall for the ruse of absolute speech rights, which have never existed in our country's history, to force people to prove their humanity 165 years after Frederick Douglass refused to do so.

4

WHAT "SNOWFLAKES" GET

RIGHT ABOUT FREE SPEECH

AT[1] ONE OF THE PREMIERES of his landmark Holocaust documentary, *Shoah* (1985), the filmmaker Claude Lanzmann was challenged by a member of the audience, a woman who identified herself as a Holocaust survivor. Lanzmann listened politely as the woman recounted her harrowing personal account of the Holocaust to make the point that the film failed to fully represent the recollections of survivors. When she finished, Lanzmann waited a bit, and then said, "Madame, you are an experience, but not an argument."

This exchange, conveyed to me by the Russian literature scholar Victor Erlich some years ago, has stayed with me, and it has taken on renewed significance as the struggles on American campuses to negotiate issues of free speech have intensified—most recently in protests at Auburn University against a visit by the white nationalist Richard Spencer.

Lanzmann's blunt reply favored reasoned analysis over personal memory. In light of his painstaking research into the Holocaust, his comment must have seemed insensitive but necessary at the time. Ironically, *Shoah* eventually helped

[1] This chapter first appeared in the *New York Times*, as part of "The Stone," April 24, 2017.

usher in an era of testimony that elevated stories of trauma to a new level of importance, especially in cultural productions and universities.

During the 1980s and 1990s, a shift occurred in American culture; personal experience and testimony, especially of suffering and oppression, began to challenge the primacy of argument. Freedom of expression became a flash point in this shift. Then as now, both liberals and conservatives were wary of the privileging of personal experience, with its powerful emotional impact, over reason and argument, which some fear will bring an end to civilization, or at least to freedom of speech.

We should resist the temptation to rehash these debates. Doing so would overlook the fact that a thorough generational shift has occurred. Widespread caricatures of students as overly sensitive, vulnerable, and entitled "snowflakes" fail to acknowledge the philosophical work that was carried out, especially in the 1980s and 1990s, to legitimate experience—especially traumatic experience—which had been dismissed for decades as unreliable, untrustworthy, and inaccessible to understanding.

The philosopher Jean-François Lyotard, best known for his prescient analysis in *The Postmodern Condition* of how public discourse discards the categories of true/false and just/unjust in favor of valuing the mere fact that something is being communicated, examined the tension between experience and argument in a different way.

Instead of defining freedom of expression as guaranteeing the robust debate from which the truth emerges, Lyotard focused on the asymmetry of different positions when personal experience is challenged by abstract arguments. His extreme example was Holocaust denial, where invidious but often well-publicized cranks confronted survivors with the absurd challenge to produce incontrovertible eyewitness evidence of their experience of the killing machines set up by the Nazis to exterminate the Jews of Europe. Not only was such evidence unavailable, but it also challenged the Jewish survivors to produce evidence of their own legitimacy in a discourse that had systematically denied their humanity.

Lyotard shifted attention away from the content of free speech to the way certain topics restrict speech as a public good. Additional important philosophers of democracy, such as Jürgen Habermas, Bonnie Honig, and Sheyla Benhabib, have focused on the very condition for discussing controversial questions. Some things are unmentionable and undebatable, but not because they offend the sensibilities of the sheltered young. Some topics, such as claims that some human beings are by definition inferior to others, or illegal or unworthy of legal standing, are not open to debate because such people cannot debate them on the same terms.

The recent student demonstrations at Auburn against Spencer's visit—as well as protests on other campuses against Charles Murray, Milo Yiannopoulos, and others—should be understood as an attempt to ensure the conditions of free speech for a greater group of people, rather than censorship. Liberal free-speech advocates rush to point out that the views of these individuals must be heard first to be rejected. But this is not the case. Universities invite speakers not chiefly to present otherwise unavailable discoveries, but to present to the public views they have presented elsewhere. When those views invalidate the humanity of some people, they restrict speech as a public good.

In such cases there is no inherent value to be gained from debating them in public. In today's age, we also have a simple solution that should appease all those concerned that students are insufficiently exposed to controversial views. It is called the internet, where all kinds of offensive expression flourish unfettered on a vast platform available to nearly all.

The great value and importance of freedom of expression, for higher education and for democracy, is hard to underestimate. But it has been regrettably easy for commentators to create a simple dichotomy between a younger generation's oversensitivity and free speech as an absolute good that leads to the truth. We would do better to focus on a more sophisticated understanding, such as the one provided by Lyotard, of the necessary conditions for speech to be a common, public good. This requires the realization that in politics, the parameters of public speech must be continually redrawn to accommodate those who previously had no standing.

The rights of transgender people for legal equality and protection against discrimination are a current example in a long history of such redefinitions. It has been a long struggle, based on truly critical scholarship that has resulted in changes not only in understanding and policy but also terminology, to change dominant ways of thinking in this context from rejecting people labeled as deficient to accepting fellow human beings. It is only when trans people are recognized as fully human, rather than as men and women in disguise, as Ben Carson, the current secretary of housing and urban development claims, that their rights can be fully recognized in policy decisions.

The idea of freedom of speech does not mean a blanket permission to say anything anybody thinks. It means balancing the inherent value of a given view with the obligation to ensure that other members of a given community can participate in discourse as fully recognized members of that community. Free-speech protections—not only but especially in universities, which aim to educate students in how to belong to various communities—should not mean that someone's humanity, or their right to participate in political speech as political agents, can be freely attacked, demeaned, or questioned.

The student activism that has roiled campuses— at Auburn, Missouri, Yale, Berkeley, Middlebury, and elsewhere—is an opportunity to take stock of free speech issues in a changed world. It is also an opportunity to take into account the past few decades of scholarship that has honed our understanding of the rights to expression in higher education, which maintains particularly high standards of what is worthy of debate.

The recent controversies over the conflict between freedom of expression and granting everyone access to speech hark back to another telling moment. In 1963, Yale University had rescinded an invitation to Alabama's segregationist governor, George C. Wallace. In 1974, after unruly protests prevented William Shockley from debating his recommendation for voluntary sterilization of people with low IQs, and other related incidents, Yale issued a report on how best to uphold the value of free speech on campus that remains the gold standard for many other institutions.

Unlike today's somewhat reflexive defenders of free speech, the Yale report situated the issue of free speech on campus within the context of an increasingly inclusive university and the changing demographics of society at large. While Yale bemoaned the occasional "paranoid intolerance" of student protesters, the university also criticized the "arrogant insensitivity" of free speech advocates who failed to acknowledge that requiring of someone in public debate to defend their human worth conflicts with the community's obligation to assure all of its members equal access to public speech.

In the 1980s and 1990s, it was universities that gave room to philosophical thinking, though not necessarily in departments bearing that name, which acknowledged the claims of people who had not been granted full participation in public discourse. Their accounts, previously dismissed as "unspeakable" or "unimaginable," now gained legitimacy in redefining the rules of what counts as public speech. Lyotard taught at Yale in the early 1990s, and his and others' thoughts on how to resolve the asymmetry in discussions between perpetrators and victims of systemic or personal violence, without curtailing speech too much, seeped into other disciplines.

Lyotard and others were interested in expanding the frames of discourse, as they had been before, when married women were granted full legal status after centuries of having their very being legally suspended upon marriage.

When Yale issued its guidelines about free speech, it did so, as did many other institutions that proudly committed to expanding their horizons, to account for a new reality, in the early 1970s, when increasing numbers of minority students and women enrolled at elite college campuses. We live in a new reality as well. We should recognize that the current generation of students, roundly ridiculed by an unholy alliance of so-called alt-right demagogues and campus liberals as coddled snowflakes, realized something important about this country before the pundits and professors figured it out.

What is under severe attack, in the name of an absolute notion of free speech, are the opportunities and real options beyond an empty promise of minorities to participate in public discourse. The snowflakes sensed, a good year before the election of President Trump, that insults and direct threats could once again become sanctioned by the most powerful office in the land. They grasped that racial and sexual equality is not so deep in the DNA of the American public that even some of its legal safeguards could not be undone.

The issues to which the students are so sensitive might be benign when they occur within the ivory tower. Coming from the campaign trail and now the White House, the threats are not meant to merely offend. Like President Trump's attacks on the liberal media as the "enemies of the American people," his insults are meant to discredit and delegitimize whole groups as less worthy of participation in the public exchange of ideas.

As a college professor and university administrator with over two decades of direct experience of campus politics, I am not overly worried that even the shrillest heckler's vetoes will end free speech in America. As a scholar of literature, history, and politics, I am especially attuned to the next generation's demands to revise existing definitions of free speech to accommodate previously delegitimized experiences. Freedom of expression is not an unchanging absolute. When its proponents forget that it requires the vigilant and continuing examination of its parameters, and instead invoke a pure model of free speech that has never existed, the dangers to our democracy are clear and present.

We should thank the student protestors, the activists in Black Lives Matter, and other "overly sensitive" souls for keeping watch over the soul of our republic.

5

AN UNHOLY ALLIANCE

What Liberals and Conservatives Mean When They Defend Free Speech in the University

> If it is a world you want, then strict justice is impossible. And if it is strict justice you want, then a world is impossible.
>
> B'RESHIT RABBA (300–500 C.E.) 49: 20

IN THE MANY DEBATES ABOUT free speech on college campuses, free speech absolutists from both sides of the political spectrum have united to defend a great American ideal. Both conservatives and progressives, from Fox News to *New York* magazine, and from neo-Nazis to *The Atlantic Monthly*, advocate absolute speech rights on campus against what they view as the encroachment of this right by overly sensitive students and censorious, timid administrators. Universities should be obligated to uphold this bedrock principle of American democracy at any cost, self-styled absolutists maintain, except when it incites imminent violence. In a period when the proverbial aisle between political factions seems like an unbridgeable chasm, it is reassuring that people of divergent political stripes rally around this foundational right, often viewed as the wellspring for all other liberties. Behind the apparent consensus, however, lurk two quite different conceptions of speech rights. In order to settle speech issues in universities in a coherent and consistent way, it is critical to understand the difference between these underlying principles.

FREE SPEECH IS INNATE TO HUMAN FLOURISHING

Why does an absolute principle of freedom of expression unite otherwise diametrically opposed groups? Why is free speech regarded as a sacred right never to be curtailed in our nation, while the government may even take the life of a citizen, as long as due process is protected? At first blush, free speech is so vigorously defended by all sides of the political spectrum because we all speak. Speech laws that shape our conception and exercise of speech even in contexts not directly shaped by court opinion, including the First Amendment and local statutes, uphold what philosopher Simone Weil called, in a commissioned report written in 1943 on the options of restoring democracy to France after the German occupation, "a fundamental need for human flourishing." Our nation's Founders wisely enshrined this need, which Benjamin Franklin called a "principal pillar of a free government," as an inalienable right not to be suppressed by the state. Since everyone experiences the need for self-expression on a visceral, personal, and existential level before it reaches the realm of politics and law, everyone agrees that the right to speak his or her mind—which is, in the first instance, his or her *personal* speech—should be unrestricted. I am an American and my government should not be allowed to punish me for anything

I say. Conservatives and progressives share this definition of speech as innate to human flourishing.

But speech does not happen in a vacuum. It is a social activity intended to affect others, and, like all human liberties, it requires certain conditions to be met so that all persons may exercise this right. In limited public institutions, such as universities, speech occurs in the service of a specific mission, which is education and the advancement of knowledge. Many commentators, both in technical legal discussions and the largely unregulated court of public opinion, agree on the conditions that undergird speech rights. Ideas should be tested in a robust and open-ended debate; truth should grapple with falsehood; restriction of speech will lead to a slippery slope of more governmental repression; all ideas are potentially valuable; offensive speech, like germs strengthening our immune system, keeps citizens from becoming coddled and fosters society's capacity for toleration. Lastly, free speech is cited not only as the basis "for all other well-being of mankind," in J. S. Mill's famous words dating to 1859, but as a democratic right especially worth defending today, in an era when politics has become polarized, tough conversations difficult, and democratic norms and even laws seem in peril.

A RARE MOMENT OF CONSENSUS: WE ALL BELIEVE IN FREE SPEECH

But if writers from *Breitbart News* to *The Atlantic Monthly* agree on absolute speech rights, and if we assume, as I do, that all of them are primarily interested in the greater good, why are we living through a series of crises over speech? The easy answer is that the current generation of students has not yet learned to appreciate the hallowed history of our First Amendment, and that they are willing to sacrifice a critical ingredient of democratic life over minor issues of no consequence, namely their wish not to be offended. This framing of extremist speech as offending feelings is a misconception. Rather than being right or wrong a priori, the students draw our attention to the ways in which the bi-partisan defense of absolute speech rights rests on different principles. In our politically polarized moment, when other norms of behavior which define a democracy seem up for grabs, absolute speech rights allow people who disagree on fundamental issues to reassure each other of their commitment to America's foundational principles. What is papered over in this unholy alliance is the fact that conservative and progressive mean different things when they say free speech. Many people think that despite all of our political differences, at least we can all agree on free speech. This rare consensus should encourage us to leave the matter alone. But both conceptions require additional nuance before they can be applied to the limited public setting of the university. When examined more closely, the right and the left have quite different reasons for attaching themselves to absolutes. And in their differences, when they defend the absolute speech rights for speakers peddling pseudo-scientific theories in the context of the university, both sides are often wrong.

The Relativism at the Heart of Free Speech Absolutism

Shouldn't all voices be heard, regardless of considerations of power, social realities, and past grievances? When he directly threaten the liberty of others. Society, in this conception which explains free speech as one of the most important mechanisms for expression autonomy, in Susan Williams' useful taxonomy, is the righteous struggle of individuals vying for advantage. The role of government is to protect individuals from the inclinations of economically, politically, or physically stronger people or groups to overwhelm the weak. This social contract to ensure everyone's safety must be drawn as narrowly as possible, so that all are safe while all maintain the greatest degree of liberty. Conservatives' full-throated defense of absolute speech rights on college campuses, which are limited public places that receive federal support and must protect all federally guaranteed rights, rests on a fear of governmental suppression of some viewpoints. Their assumption is that colleges ought to be perfect instances of the marketplace of ideas where various opinions jostle for dominance, and that all members of that community have access to it as long as the government does not prevent them. No ground rules are needed for this competitive environment, since any rule would favor one viewpoint over others. If a speaker denies some students their right of equal access to the space, by questioning their status as full human beings, those students or faculty should skip the event, toughen up, or counter this idea with more speech. The risk of losing a potentially valid viewpoint, even when cloaked in noxious language, is always greater than not hearing even the most extreme position on campus. The assumption is that nobody can decide now whether some idea might be useful in the future, which means it must be presented for all to discuss.

Generally speaking, conservatives do not accept the idea that speech can undermine the equality principle which is required in today's university to carry out its mission. There is also little explicit acknowledgment of the central purpose of universities, which accepts as expert consensus that some problems have been settled and need not be revisited again. The speech rights guaranteed by the current interpretations of the First Amendment, which permit restrictions to prevent incitement, obscenity, treason, or libelous harm, and limit the use of "fighting words" and deliberate falsehoods leading to harm, such as falsely yelling fire in a crowded theater, are accepted as the only valid ground rules.

The conservative definition of absolute speech rights on campus amount to a strong defense of individualism and autonomy. But it is an abstract and rather limited conception of the individual outside of a specific social or political context, modeled on Jean-Jacques Rousseau's mythic notion of natural man before civilization, who innately experiences his freedom but is then subjected to the rules of society, where others who have equal demands for their freedom curtail his liberty. For this argument to work, aside from having to suspend one's knowledge of both modern anthropology and political science, specific instances of speech must be turned into the abstract notion of a "right to offend." Among them are calls for a white ethno-state, the argument to eliminate minorities from the public, or the identification of a student based on his or her group identity to a hostile audience. There is no need—in fact it is outrageous, spurious, and unnecessary—for a balancing of interests to assuage the fears of those wanting to protect hate speech in particular. It might be intellectually satisfying to engage in such an exercise. But none of the statements proposed by these groups, that is, calling for the elimination, degradation, or subordination of a group's humanity, has an equivalence on the "other side of the ideological spectrum." There is no direct equivalence, or similarity in merit, of such groups with the views of other political groups like Black Lives Matter, women's rights groups, or other minority interest groups whose advocacy is based on advancing the fundamental American principle of equality while a hate group like the alt-right does the exact opposite. Importantly, hate-based groups deny minority members the right to participate in the political process, including open and robust debate. They seek to invalidate the rules to which all must adhere, while groups advocating for equality might challenge existing structures but do not seek to destroy the rules for debate. Humans have a tendency to use intemperate speech, and no one has the authority to interfere with this penchant unless it imminently incites violence. Conservatives hesitate to label particular speech as injurious or hateful, since even virulent racism or misogyny may just be a personal opinion, rooted in a speaker's inalienable right to hold personal views.

This move is critical, from considering the specific situation of enrolled students and invited speakers with known positions in a lecture hall to abstractly discussing the risks of state suppression of speech, from specific arguments about racial inferiority, lesser humans, the supremacy of a white master race, or men over women, to an abstract discussion of any person's constitutionally guaranteed freedom to invite dispute without state suppression. This last point, when framed in purely technical terms as allowing people to express themselves without censorship, is something with which few will disagree.

Students have challenged this way of framing the actual threats to their equal access to the educational setting as an abstract matter of legal principles to be decided by the courts. They do not accept the practice of deliberately ignoring the specific circumstances of hateful speakers on a college campus, of turning isolated incidents into narratives of cultural decline, premised on an Edenic earlier state where minorities knew their place was acceptance of the status quo. They do not accept as the only solution the practice of adjudicating those cases only in theory, which turns every neo-Nazi and hard-core pornographer into a free speech apostle defending our country's fundamental freedoms, and depicts those asking for equality as child-like, ignorant, or censorial traitors. Indeed, students criticize the practice of leaping over our country's political history and over the particular purpose of the university, which has admitted diverse students in earnest, that is, in more significant if still inadequate numbers, for the past 50 years but continues to uphold unequal conditions. If they are faulted for politicizing the university, they reply that the idea of the university's position outside of politics is a comforting illusion, but an illusion nonetheless. The Nazis do not come to campus to lecture on the First Amendment. They promote an agenda of destroying the possibility of open debate.

Students notice a problem in the strategy of not identifying the content of speech, through recourse to the abstract exercise of viewpoint neutrality (with the exceptions noted above). But this rigidly abstract effort to judge speech without consideration of both meaning and context does not work for the university. There, teaching means more than exposure to a jumble of facts, opinions, and ideas. It means imparting the skills of telling falsehood from truth, privileging argument over force, and elevating evidence-based reason over personal opinion. On college campuses, speech matters precisely because it has a specific meaning.

Its particular message is indeed why speakers are invited. Otherwise it is at best a distraction, entertainment, or simply noise. Speech absolutists invoke "viewpoint neutrality" as if it were a self-explanatory rather than complicated legal principle with widely disparate interpretations. With this sleight-of-hand they turn the advocacy of inequality, which undermines the university's purpose and functioning, into a generic matter of debating competing viewpoints with which everyone, on the face of it, agrees.

THE RISKS OF SUPPRESSING HATE

The greatest danger to speech, in the conservative view, arrives not in the form of bad ideas or, as J. S. Mill maintained, from the oppressive force of the court of public opinion today found on-line, but from state suppression. Since the government has unrivaled means of force, once it starts limiting personal freedoms there are no other agents to keep things from going down a slippery slope toward totalitarian rule. The idea is that the state, which holds the monopoly on and has the greatest means of violent coercion, must not invade any citizen's private realm. Originally this area had been a matter of religious faith, and it is a major tenet of American society that the government should not dictate anyone's belief. But in today's age, religion plays a less dominant or at least less visible role in public life than it had in the founding days of the Republic. In public institutions such as universities, the original prohibition on the government to invade anyone's private realm, or what is still called a person's conscience, shifts to the protection of free speech. In contemporary society, abortion." In the "Mexico City policy," a US government policy that has been enacted by all Republican presidents since Ronald Reagan in 1984, rescinded by all Democratic presidents, and was re-instituted by President Trump on his first day in office, the use of language "on abortion" is strictly forbidden to be used by any non-governmental organizations with federal funding. Such language is not permitted, even though this is, without a doubt, a content-based restriction of speech based on what lawmakers otherwise reject as an unacceptable basis for speech regulation. A Supreme Court ruling in 2018 affirmed the right to restrict language on abortion in faith-based clinics even when they receive public funding. In these cases and in the presidential order, the right of speech, which has come to occupy in secular society the place formerly reserved for religious belief, is trumped by the right to religious freedom, here expressed as supporting the overriding sanctity of life. In modern society, where religion pervades public life and political discourse to a lesser extent than during earlier periods, conservative lawmakers defend religious belief even when this means that the government directly restricts speech. This is no different from the government allowing the restriction of pro-choice advocates to speak at a public university or to mention abortion in the student health center. By prohibiting speech about a legally permissible procedure, they are doing exactly what they decry as unconstitutional when a college declines to host a white supremacist. The point is not, or not only, that the conservative support for direct governmental speech restrictions, for instance in the Mexico City policy and the Supreme Court's recent decisions, is inconsistent and, if you will, hypocritical. Rather, conservatives make an exception to their otherwise absolute stance on free speech when it comes to a more explicit religious matter, which is what they define as the right to life. In this case, they opt for protecting that matter rather than protecting the individual's freedom of speech from government suppression. This is why student groups at Notre Dame opposed a commencement address by Barack Obama in 2009 and, joined by religious leaders and some faculty, a visit by Joe Biden in 2016, in spite of the university's commitment to free speech. They considered these invitations to pro-choice advocates offensive to their beliefs. The Mexico City policy, and other restrictions on speech for religious schools, indicate that conservatives know that speech matters. They are fully aware that without viewpoint distinction, speech rights have no traction, and that despite their insistence that all ideas must be permitted, they accept restrictions on speech when it conflicts with what they consider other more fundamental values.

SELF-GOVERNANCE AS A LIMIT TO BAD IDEAS

Conservatives, the vast differences among them notwithstanding, regard the public as a tough but ultimately equal playing field, which all Americans enter with the same birthright for speech that the government must not suppress. They reject, or at least vociferously proclaim to do so, nearly any regulation of speech as an inappropriate governmental interference. They are aware of the danger that some speech can undermine the workings of democracy itself. Why is this a risk worth entertaining? Conservatives believe we can go this far and permit speech that is anti-democratic (even if they seek to restrict expression they define as un-American) because there is one innate limit to speech. On the side of the individual, there is an innate capacity for "virtuous self-governance," which is also often called civility, morality, or respect. A seminal expression of this notion of "self-governance" is found in James Madison's *Federalist Paper* 55, published under the pseudonym *Publius* in 1788, to promote the ratification of our Constitution. Madison explained that American society can forgo authoritarian rule in favor of republicanism, as a form of government, which lacks the absolute power to restrain people's worst impulses, because we Americans presuppose "the existence of [. . .] sufficient virtue among men for self-government." "Republican government," which for Madison meant our American system of a representative rather than direct democracy, "presupposes the existence of [qualities in human nature which justify a certain portion of esteem and confidentiality] in a higher degree than [depravity]."

The idea is that Americans can be granted as much freedom as possible because the slight preponderance of virtue over vice functions as an internal safety valve that will prevent them from "destroying and devouring one another." It is safe to grant everyone absolute speech rights, according to Madison and contemporary First Amendment absolutists, since people will be prohibited by their innate capacity for self-governance from exercising their right to say the worst. Secondly, the structure of a representative democracy will prevent passion from wresting "the scepter from reason," which Madison considered inevitable in all numerous assemblies. The contemporary, secular counterpart to the notion of virtuous "self-governance" is the idea of innate civility. Decent conduct and respect are touted by conservative scholars and commentators as the individual's innate capacity to sacrifice rash and rude behavior in order to live together. Teresa Bejan usefully distinguishes the ubiquitous talk about civility, which frequently serves to silence others, from "mere civility," which she defines as courageous disagreement that does not preclude a common life for the two parties. The crux, encapsulated in Madison's faith that the good qualities of Americans outweigh the bad, is that as Americans, we do not need governmental guardrails even on speech that could bring the republic down, since we are restrained by our inherent virtue, by the preponderance of good over evil in our pluralistic society, from promoting such ideas.

By relying on the individual's innate capacity to choose virtue over vice, one can dismiss as unnecessary any enabling conditions that would guarantee the same rights for all. Let everyone argue for his or her freedom, and since all Americans taken as whole, in Madison's view, have an inborn penchant for liberty, all will end up free. What does this mean for the university? Conservatives expect universities to fund platforms for all speakers, since even the most noxious speakers, intent on destroying discourse; invalidating reason, argument, and mutual respect; and undermining the public good of a well-ordered society, will be overcome by the greater number of those who advocate tolerance, open-mindedness, and love. For conservatives, the worst they can imagine is state suppression of a viewpoint, which Madison called "the chains of despotism," given that vice will be either resisted by the speaker or overcome by the majority of virtuous citizens.

THE PROGRESSIVE CASE
FOR UNRESTRICTED SPEECH

Many liberals, the vast differences among them notwith-standing, generally defend free speech as an absolute ideal not primarily to expand the reach of individual liberty, although they cherish liberty as well. They advocate for absolute speech rights on campus for two main reasons. First, liberals worry that restrictions on speech will eventually limit them. "We do so not because we support hateful speech, but because our founders understood that without such protections, the capacity of each individual to express their own views . . . may be threatened," President Barack Obama stated at the United Nations in 2012. History indeed offers examples of progressive viewpoints being suppressed by authorities. In this slippery slope argument, once government restricts one form of speech, it will not curb its own power in a succession of black-robed judges and democratically elected legislators, but restrict more and more speech. While conservatives worry about big government in general, liberals worry about bad government specifically.

THE TRUTH WILL ALWAYS PREVAIL

But liberals defend free speech with narrow exceptions so vigorously because they believe that the open debate of diverging ideas will vanquish falsehoods and bad ideas to yield the truth. Susan Williams distinguishes this conception from the "autonomy theory" because it prioritizes the idea that free speech is one of the best means for human discovery of the truth. This truth, for liberals, is not simply a particularly apt worldview but a better outcome. Robust debate is the engine of progress. While justice, equality, and freedom for all may be difficult to achieve, the truth that these principles are the best will ultimately prevail. They defend the rights to extremist speech, which they abhor, to profess their unwavering and noble principles. Defending the neo-Nazis is proof of their moral fortitude. They also believe that disputes will be settled on the basis of what is *true, reasonable, and just*, rather than what is persuasive, popular, better phrased, or backed by force. Extremist positions, progressive speech advocates maintain, will be defeated in the marketplace of ideas, which extends all around the college lectern, by refutation, reasoned critique, or ridicule. The Nazis will be laughed out of the lecture hall; the Holocaust deniers will scurry off when their lies are examined in the light of day; the racial supremacists will recognize the wrongness of assaulting the dignity of minorities and the rightness of America's bedrock principle of equality, once they've been exposed to reasoned argument and more speech from the other side. More speech! This, liberals hope, will yield the truth. Even the most talented demagogue, wielding seductive falsehoods with the elegance of a samurai's sword, will yield to reason and the truth when faced by better arguments. Progressives believe, as the ACLU's David Cole maintains, that "free speech allows us to resolve our differences through public reason."

In their faith in the inevitability of progress, progressives fail to recognize that contradiction, falsehood, or stupidity do not necessarily discredit a speaker. They also fail to see that engaging with bigoted and hateful speakers often gives those speakers what they want and boosts "their need and sense of entitlement that drives them in the first place," rather than refute them, as Kate Manne explains in *Down*

Girl, her study of misogyny. When a speaker goes low by singling out students in the lecture hall as less than human, mocking disabled visitors, or denigrating women as objects, liberals go high. But in the realm of politics and perhaps in the public sphere in general, these elegant rules of argument which privilege truth over falsehood, coherence over confusion, facts over feelings, evidence over experience, and analysis over anecdote, have never fully applied. Successful politicians who flout the rules of civility and instead demean and insult others are proof that political speech does not have to be truthful, honest, or reasonable to be effective. With their faith in the inevitable march of reason, liberals overlook that the public is as or even more easily swayed by a speaker who breaks taboos, tells it "like it is," denies proven facts, and eschews reason with a sufficiently loud microphone, since people may be persuaded by things other than evidence, reason, and the sober truth. Instead of taking to heart the Aristotelian delineation of the different registers of speech, of which truthfulness, or *logos*, is only one besides emotion, or *pathos*, liberals call for reasonable speech to defeat what they view as unreason.

In defending absolute speech rights, since the unfettered airing of noxious ideas will presumably bring out the truth, many progressives defend their core belief, or at least their animating hope: that humanity is on a one-way path, however twisted and rocky it may be, toward moral progress. For them, the truth wins out because it is good *in essence* and inevitable, and not because someone presented an argument with better phrasing, was more charismatic, was backed by power and resources, or encountered favorable conditions. Carol Christ, Chancellor of the University of California at Berkeley, invokes John Stuart Mill to affirm her faith in truth's innate force: "The first is that truth is of such power that it will always ultimately prevail; any abridgement of argument therefore compromises the opportunity of exchanging error for truth."

Liberals place our fate in the hands of reasoned discourse, because reason will win out. They may have an exceedingly dark view of human nature and the arc of history, but unfettered speech seems the only viable remedy to forestall the worst. Indeed, speech, which they align with reason and truth, seems to harbor the possibility of light, even if action, most likely, is what prompted progress. It might be a rocky ride for some, but with a sufficiently thick skin and a few political bruises, and the option to stay home when the Nazis come to town, everyone will be better off in the end, as long as we grant a hearing to even the worst ideas. In fact, exposure to hateful ideas will increase society's overall capacity for the toleration of difference.

Liberals, even with the many differences and stark controversies among them, make a basic assumption that all speakers are committed to the idea of open debate in order to winnow out the truth. This happens to be the operating principle of the university. It is the price of admission into the academic space, so to speak. But when someone has a record of eschewing the rules of debate, of lying deliberately in order to undermine others' faith in reason, and refusing the overall goal of reaching a consensus on truth and falsehoods, any rented hall but not the university is a perfect setting for his or her speech. The liberal commitment to reason is admirable. It is also politically naïve. It assumes that in the plurality of values found in our society, there are no speakers who dispute and want to destroy the values of debate, argument, and reason. It assumes that the marketplace of ideas in itself is not a political value but an unchanging, neutral pre-condition. It assumes that reason and truth have self-enforcing powers. It assumes that going low can only be defeated by going high. It assumes that reason can win out over force in all situations unless, liberals say by clinging to an abstract and overly legalistic assessment of the university's obligation to keep everyone safe, when an actual weapon or fist is making actual contact with a listener. But when there is a threat of force prompted by speech that marks individuals as lesser humans, even when no gun has yet been drawn, such speech has already crossed a line beyond the educational mission. With their faith in reason, liberals fail to recognize a move that checkmates the university each time and that lets virulent extremists always win by default. This happens when speakers come not to present an argument but to score symbolic victories, and to gain legitimacy for their cause, either by ascending a college stage or by becoming a martyr of First Amendment suppression.

THE CALL FOR TOLERANCE

Many liberals further maintain that once a level of freedom and equality has been attained, it is difficult to backslide. In the college context, this assumption has particular significance. Are there ideas that undermine the very conditions for debate in ways that cannot simply be restored with more speech? It is important to underline again that universities must have ground rules to operate. One of those rules is that robust debate will not lead to the abolition of the university itself, nor to the abolition of its essential commitment to equal participation. Are there ideas to this effect that cannot be countered with reason? What about speakers who do not respect the truth, who aim to undermine the role of experts, and who spread lies for their own sake in order to sow confusion? Or is the imminence of violence the only threat and acceptable reason to regulate the exchange of ideas in a university lecture hall?

When racial supremacists visit college to advocate against some students' innate right to exist, liberals such as Timothy Garton Ash, in an admirably and impressively comprehensive global study of free speech that, strangely, omits any discussion of equality, counsel 18-year olds to turn the other cheek à la Mahatma Gandhi, James Baldwin, Nelson Mandela, or other pacifist revolutionaries. It is laudable and powerful counsel to reason with one's enemies and give them the benefit of the doubt, even if none of the leaders cited by Ash believed—not Gandhi, not Baldwin, not Mandela—that speech alone, without coordinated group action, can defeat race-based inequality. But the question is whether views that dispute the full humanity of some people will reliably be defeated by reason in humanity's inevitably progress. It might be the case, as Supreme Court Justice Robert Jackson put it in a dissenting opinion about speech ridiculing religious belief in *Kunz v. New York* (1951), that some statements "do not spring from reason and *can be answered by none*" (emphasis added). What argument can refute a speaker who excludes some people from the debate *on principle*, by declaring them on the basis of group affiliation as inherently inferior, unfit for higher education, or not worthy of life?

When such ideas are afforded a platform in the limited public institution of a university, as liberals demand in the name of fostering robust debate and viewpoint neutrality, some students and faculty are forced to make an ontological claim about their humanity, while others grapple with academic ideas. Through the history of our country and in many universities, especially minority and female students have met this demand of proving their existence, with tremendous poise and courage on a daily basis. In *Upending the Ivory Tower*, Stefan Bradley shows how Black students in particular transformed American higher education through courageous action long before any white administrators or politicians recognized their claims. They have also found ways of refusing this demand, and challenging it as an undue imposition. Some celebrate such instances of truly free speech which occur in spite of and against a doctrinaire understanding of absolute speech rights, as the triumph of reason. I regard them as proof that progress cannot be taken for granted but must be achieved through the continual adaptation of our institutions to serve an evolving population.

Instead of staking my hope on inevitable progress or the capacity of toleration, this is the place where I see a slippery slope. The tax-payer-funded promotion of ideas of some groups' inherent inferiority violates constitutional rights and core American values, namely the interlocking principles of liberty and equality. By bestowing on such speech the prestige of a university, we do not ensure automatic progress through the inevitable elimination of such ideas, but force students to abandon debate and instead testify to the worth of their existence. It is those ideas, rather than the regulation of speech in limited public institutions which the law has always been willing to consider, that undo America's greatest achievements even when a speaker does not bring a noose or a gun to the lectern.

Many liberals respond that the unregulated market-place of ideas, as long as it is free from violence, is still our best option. They argue that if we institute any ground rules, if a line were to be drawn, soon only the most inoffensive ideas would be expressible. Soon thereafter, our liberal views would be suppressed. But this idea that the status quo is neutral, that we exist in a static and empty social space, ignores that the conditions of the proverbial marketplace, like a newspaper's editorial guidelines, the rules and procedures of Congress, or the behavior around your dinner table, or, indeed, like the rules of an actual market, must be and are agreed upon, even when and if they are re-negotiated. Conservatives sometimes insert the idea of "self-governance" here, which in fact often shields powerful private actors from any such rule. Equally loath to invite governmental regulation, most liberals insist that ultimately reason will triumph in the battle of ideas.

Even our nation's bedrock truth that "all men are created equal," some will object, was the result of careful deliberation and reasoned debate! Not so. The conditions of equality that turn free speech into the glue of democracy were established not in an unregulated marketplace of ideas, such as the Constitutional Convention, where truth tussled with falsehood. Jefferson and Franklin penned the phrase to break with the British, not to continue a dialogue and see which viewpoint wins out. They bristled at being governed without consent by a far-away monarch and insisted on their right to self-determination. Ultimate snowflakes that they were, they were triggered by the very notion of *inherent* inequality. They were enraged by the suggestion that they were inherently inferior to those born into a higher social class (which did not prevent them from considering themselves superior to women and non-Europeans). But the belief that political inequality is justified because people are different, that people can be treated differently by their government depending on who they are, is exactly the type of idea which extremists want to bring back to campus. We know that these ideas were not refuted through debate. The Founding Fathers waged a war to insist on their political equality with those who ruled them. They did not wait for the better, self-governing angels of the British rulers' nature to set them free, and they did not stage a debate to let the truth win out, which meant either bondage or freedom. They defeated the idea of innate inequality by force, because they knew that not all ideas which exclude some people from humanity, and thus from debate, will be settled by debate. It is because the conditions for free speech had to be created by force that we must be cautious when assuming free speech simply happens on its own, hemmed in by our virtuous capacity for self-restraint, by the innate force of reason to impose itself, by a cleverly designed constitution that anticipated even leaders who ignore it, and as long as nobody draws a line and the government "makes no law" restraining it. Free speech is an inherent human need but also, anthropologists and philosophers remind us, a social activity, and as such it is necessary to establish its rules. When colleges are forced to spend enormous resources to let people speak on campus who allege the inherent inferiority of some groups, in the hope that reason will win out, they are enabling the destruction of free speech, not protecting it. I maintain that our obligation toward the sanctity of other human beings, solemnly enshrined by our laws, must not be put up for debate.

THE AMERICAN CASE FOR FREE SPEECH: SELF-GOVERNANCE AND THE FAITH IN PROGRESS

So why do so many liberals maintain their faith in the unfettered exchange of ideas as something that will result in a more just outcome? The issue is not whether it is justified to believe that the arc of history is bent toward justice. We all have a right to have hope. But we should be concerned when liberals make common cause with conservatives, who do not trust that unfettered free speech will lead to a promised land of equality and freedom for all. Liberals believe robust debate will guard against error, but they believe that the opposite of error is not more error but progress and that the truth will prevail. A worthy principle, but little consolation for those living in the present, where the louder and more powerful voices, full of error and deliberate lies and inciting violence "with passionate intensity," while the critics "lack all conviction," as Yeats put it in his poem "The Second Coming," may carry the day.

Many conservatives, in fact, think that absolute speech rights should protect individuals against the power of the state, but they do not have unlimited faith that unfettered debate will yield the best results. In their view, quite a few topics are not open for debate. These conservatives have no quarrel with curtailing speech rights informing clients about abortion for limited public institutions that receive federal support, or to define baking cakes as a form of speech so that bakers can refuse to serve gay customer. They do not believe athletes should be allowed to express their views except in ways dictated by their employers. They accept such restrictions on speech because they believe it could under-mine another First Amendment right, namely the free ex-ercise of religion. By carving out religiously motivated restrictions on speech, conservatives defend the notion that every person is ultimately grounded in his or her innermost being rather than a product of the collective.

One purpose of universities is to activate the capacity for self-government in young people through education, rather than presuppose it. Indeed, universities teach students some-thing like democratic intuitions, which are different from legal or moral principles but can grow into the norms of be-havior necessary for a functioning social order. Universities share the belief that humanity can make progress on a basic level: they sponsor teaching and research since they believe this will contribute to a greater good. But there are strict guidelines to prevent unethical research. Not all options are tested to their extreme conclusions. In fact, the univer-sity does not operate on the assumption, as many liberals tend to proclaim, that more speech automatically enhances education. The university's assumption is not that the best ideas prevail automatically in a mosh-pit of opinions but that progress for humanity, and not the Faustian bargain of trading our values for knowledge, requires ruling out some ideas from inquiry and debate.

Both conservatives and liberals protest any regulation of speech lest it lead to government overreach. Notwithstanding the fact that speech must always adhere to some ground rules in order to remain meaningful, many people advocate ab-solute speech rights in the university because they do not believe that speech could disrupt the university's mission. Frequently, they want to push their political agenda in the name of viewpoint diversity, because they do not trust the community of academic experts to represent the positions they want to see included. With tiresome regularity, they defend especially extremist speech, often eliding the fact that such speech is frequently unscientific and disproven, because they believe that Americans are molded by their capacity for self-restraint, or they wish to impose such restraint on the people targeted by such speech. They also believe that America is proof for humanity's inevitable progress. In such debates, it rarely discussed that the status quo everyone wants to defend already includes various regulations of speech and is a result of complex legal and political decisions, rather than a God-given state of nature. The people living in other democracies, where speech is regulated differently, they assert, might lack the capacity for self-governance and must accept stricter controls.

FREE SPEECH AND MORAL LEADERSHIP

Even diehard Madisonians acknowledge that today's situation is complicated. The bi-partisan defense of absolute speech rights depends on conservatives' trust that Americans possess more virtue than depravity, that no elected leader would actively undermine constitutional principles and norms, and on progressives' faith that our country's arc is bent toward justice. These presuppositions allow conservatives and progressives to uphold uncompromising speech standards, which preclude most regulation. But for such standards to exist, there needs to be general consensus that all Americans' rights will be equally protected. For such consensus to transcend the glorious plurality of opinions in America, moral leadership is essential. Such leadership requires that the leader models self-governance in his or her own behavior; otherwise the suggestion that moderation will lead to greater unity seems insincere at best. It seems safe to say that moderation is not a trait currently favored by the US administration. Things will change again, of course. But once the government flouts these principles, the implicit limitations on extreme speech are suspended.

In campus speech debates, such a uniquely bi-partisan defense of absolute speech rights amounts to a defense of the status quo. But the status quo has changed. The nation's leader exercises little self-restraint, flouts the norms of moral leadership by attacking individual citizens and the press from the position of his office, and makes unprecedented concessions to anti-democratic forces. Today, the threats to freedom of expression consist in something else besides official censorship, violence, politically correct groupthink, and offended students. The threat to freedom of expression now includes a government that breaks the unwritten social contract which undergirds our nation's free speech doctrine and grounds it in Madisonian principles of self-governance: that both individuals' and the state's actions aim at achieving a better country for all. Once this compact is broken, the faith that even the most pernicious ideas will be defeated by more ideas, and that unreason will be buried by reason, seems more tenuous.

I do not mean to suggest that we should even entertain abandoning America's strong speech protections. Quite the opposite. Whether your general commitment is liberal or conservative, there is a need to see that discussions will only help us understand the world we live in if we agree on some ground rules, rather than invoking abstract principles by rote. When our government flouts our nation's unwritten norms that allow for the most expansive speech rights in any current democracy, we must become ever more vigilant about strengthening these norms. To argue for expansive speech rights requires absolute clarity about the norms and principles that uphold such rights. Unfortunately, neither liberals nor conservatives tend to explain their underlying assumptions. Instead, they jointly wring their hands over the loss of a speech culture that they believe has served everyone equally well. Even if one remains skeptical about the tactics and claims of the identity-based movements of our times, which include, with significant distinctions and no equivalence, Black Lives Matter, #MeToo, and the identitarian support for Donald Trump, the fact is undeniable that the system has not worked in ways that let everyone feel heard. Many commentators regularly and incorrectly credit the First Amendment with ushering in social progress long before the 1920s, when it was first applied in a ruling by the Supreme Court. By presenting the First Amendment as a powerful weapon in the struggle to win equality for all Americans, they want to encourage applying it to universities. They also suggest, in a move that political theorist Judith Shklar criticized as "legalism," which incorrectly maintains that the rules of reasoned discourse are not political in nature, that contemporary jurisprudence has the final word on the matter.

What is left out of these accounts is the link among speech, power, and equality, which the court has regularly recognized as a significant factor even in public life, and which serves an indispensable function in the university's daily operation. Without uncovering the underlying assumptions of free speech absolutism, we will not understand that the point is not simply one of defending individual liberty against the powerful state.

Scholars and commentators on both sides of the aisle resort to circular reasoning proclaiming that speech rights are fundamentally American, and that it's fundamentally American to have speech rights. Routinely, and without evidence, since it would have to be counter-factual, both liberals and conservatives declare that our nation's *current* jurisprudence is the best option to protect individual liberties in a democracy. They dismiss as inferior Canadian, British, French, South African, Indian, Brazilian, Australian, German, Italian, and countless other democracies' ways of ensuring speech rights for the greatest number of people while honoring equality and dignity. It is safe to assume that most Americans, though with varying degrees of conviction, consider today's assumptions about free speech as a right innate to non-white Americans and women, to be superior to earlier periods in American history when speech rights were limited to white men who owned property. This should be reason enough to consider whether the unquestioning embrace of contemporary speech rights, different from past practices, future legal rulings, and other democratic models, is rooted in a similar commitment to the value of equality. Strangely, a frequent response to serious interrogations of the status quo consists in enraged attacks on critics of current speech regulation as un-American doomsayers. It might simply be that the fact of minorities claiming equal rights, which is to enter debate without having to defend their moral standing, is too threatening to the status quo. But self-styled absolutists insist that all topics, *especially* including virulent hate speech, must be debated at all costs, with the exception of the sacred law one must never question: their narrow definition of free speech. Are we invoking our laws to advance the principles of freedom and equality, or are we invoking the law to uphold current interpretations of the law for its own sake, as part of our First Amendment religion, when another option is not to lend full-throated support to racist, sexist, and other exclusionary speakers?

Even James Madison, who drafted an early version of the First Amendment, thought that speech rights function only because he made the assumption that "the proportion of fit characters [in America] will present . . . a greater probability of a fit choice." This assumption that America will always elect individuals who exercise moderation, are of inherently good character, and will put the interests of the common good and the Republic above personal gain and the interests of foreign powers, testifies to our nation's unrivaled optimism. It is the pre-condition of our national faith that the best result will win out, since the people engaged in debating all share the same basic values in improving everyone's lot. But this faith is tempered by Supreme Court Justice Jackson's 1949 warning, which warrants repeating: "if the Court does not temper its doctrinaire logic [of protecting speech as an abstraction] with a little practical wisdom, it will convert the constitutional Bill of Rights into a suicide pact."

In the university, the stakes are different. The framers and the courts both acknowledge that the public sphere must not be opened up completely and without any restraint to the risk of its destruction by an overly abstract application of speech rights. Universities, which serve as models of democratic co-existence, require even stronger conditions that do not destroy equal conditions for participation. Speakers at a university can agitate, anger, and provoke. But the university is always a specific context with specific goals, which the law calls the "compelling interest," of education and research. The Supreme Court has recognized, Robert Post reminds us, that "the First Amendment does not deny a university's 'authority to impose reasonable regulations compatible with that mission upon the use of its campus and facilities,' which includes 'a university's right to exclude . . . First Amendment activities that . . . substantially interfere with the opportunity of other students to obtain an education.'" All of the university's sponsored activities should correspond to these goals. At the very least, they must not directly interfere with them. When the university is forced to host a speaker with a known record of declaring that some groups or individuals are not fully human, or who espouse proven lies, the university sacrifices its educational purpose for a rigid notion of speech which seeks to destroy the conditions under which it operates.

Freedom of speech can be undone by speakers who exhibit no capacity for self-government nor believe in human progress. This is why our Founders guaranteed the right to free expression via the Bill of Rights rather than leaving it to the citizens to decide which rights apply to whom. This document, which governs speech law in our country and guides our thinking about but does not fully apply to the limited public institution of the university, "is based upon the equality of the human race. Its primal object must be to protect each human being within its jurisdiction in the free and full enjoyment of his natural rights." These words by Representative John Bingham, framer of the Fourteenth Amendment which was ratified in 1868, remind us that only equal access to speech makes speech rights a reality for all Americans.

The idea that the human race is made of innately superior and inferior subgroups is not only junk science, and un-American. Such speech also deserves no special protection over other obsolete ideas that are not granted the prestige of a university platform without contravening anyone's speech rights. The progressive faith in inevitable human progress, in the notion that truth will prevail, and the conservative faith that "virtuous sentiments" outweigh "factious tempers" among Americans, in Madison's hopeful words, are powerful. Instead of leading to a reflexive defense of absolute speech rights, which the law has never maintained and which ignores the enabling conditions needed for speech, the difference between these premises opens up a new conversation. It could be a genuinely bi-partisan conversation not about offended feelings, safe spaces, and the silencing force of identity politics, but one where the interlocking principles of our country's fundamental rights of liberty and equality become the premise for speech that is truly free and open to all.

6

A SLIPPERY SLOPE, OR WHO

IS TO DRAW THE LINE?

A GOOD NUMBER OF PEOPLE fear that by regulating speech and excluding some ideas, we hand power to individuals who might be proven wrong in the future. Let's have the public hash it out, the thinking goes, since no person is infallible in winnowing out ideas which will never be useful again. If even the wisest, most judicious, and impartial university administrator decides, her decision will set us on a slippery slope from accommodating today's sensitive students and politically correct faculty to a future dean who will censor any form of critique or dissent. If a university, as the University of Michigan, Penn State, Ohio State, and Auburn University have all done in the fall of 2017, after the violence in Charlottesville, decides not to host a white supremacist, and he fails to convince a judge that his constitutional right to speak was punished by those decisions, it will open the floodgates to wholesale censorship. What is the basis for this fear that all rights will vanish? And why does this fear of a small step inevitably leading to disaster outweigh, according to many commentators, the real cost to equality, in the form of university students, faculty, and guests who are forced by such speakers to justify their presence based on group belonging? Why would the university's role in deciding what ideas merit debate, which is its core mission, be handed to a judge or legislator, who, as the history of speech decisions attests, could have the very tendencies so feared by free speech absolutists?

THE DANGER OF REGULATING SPEECH

"The dangers of permitting the government to decide what may and may not be said," First Amendment scholar Floyd Abrams argues, "far more often than not, outweigh any benefits that may result from suppressing or punishing offensive speech." It is a fact, well-known to experts such as Abrams, that the government regularly decides what can be said in specific situations, in order not to let speech destroy the social order which it is charged to uphold. It is also the case that Abrams's sweeping pronouncement is impossible to prove, which claims that tolerating offensive speech has invariably "outweighed" the benefit derived from regulating it. Throughout our nation's history, the courts have recognized some limitations on speech. It is difficult to claim, and by no means certain, that these limitations always damaged, rather than protected the public from violence, grave disorder, or other material attacks. Do victims of the Klan's violence agree that protecting this organization's speech rights was a benefit? Did protecting anti-suffragist speech help to grant rights to female citizens of this country? Has the protection of violent pornography on speech grounds advanced the equality and freedom of women? Did the U.S. Supreme Court's decades-long practice of limiting communist speech damage the country, or did it protect those democratic institutions, including the Court, which communists hoped to overturn? It seems that protecting speech does not always result in beneficial outcomes, or that the question of who benefits from permitting or regulating speech, remains a matter of debate. To use another example, did permitting Adolf Hitler to speak after he had been forbidden from political agitation in the 1920s, and permitting the Nazis to promulgate anti-democratic ideals in 1930's Germany through marches and speeches, provide a benefit to the world?

EXPOSURE TO HATE SPEECH BUILDS RESILIENCE

Other scholars believe that being exposed to offensive speech is an inherent benefit by strengthening resilience and inoculating against bigotry. Lee Bollinger, the advocate and champion of educational equality, argues that unrestricted exposure to hate speech in particular leads to the "increase in our capacity for toleration generally." Nadine Strossen, president emerita of the ACLU, entertains the idea that "hearing hateful speech . . . [can constitute] opportunities for positive personal development," and asserts that speech regulation in other democracies has "disproportionately suppressed dissenting views and disempowered speakers." But there is no evidence that our society has grown more tolerant because hate was permitted to flourish. I also cannot locate evidence that hate speech always provides opportunities for positive development for minority communities, or as, Strossen claims, that "hateful, discriminatory expression and actions now are swiftly and

strongly condemned by government officials." More importantly, there is no evidence (since there is not a single way
of measuring) that protecting hate speech in particular has
led to what Strossen, Abrams, and others argue, which is
less tolerance for hateful views, more equality, and a more
robust commitment to democratic principles. There is no
evidence that speech laws disproportionately suppress powerless speakers in democracies around the world, nor in the
United States. Any such claim would have to tally up direct
governmental suppression of speech in addition to social
ostracism of some ideas, and not only list a handful of puz-
zling legal decisions which exist in any area of the law. In
today's world, various hate groups, neo-Nazis, and the Klan,
all claim that they have been "disempowered" by liberal democracy. They insist on speech rights from the position of
disenfranchised victims. For the context of the university,
Strossen believes that exposing especially students from historically marginalized groups to hate speech is part of "the
rigorous education they deserve," because such exposure
will make them grow. She expresses a widely shared sentiment, disputed by scholars such as Natasha Warikoo and
Liana Garces, that exposure to injurious speech is good for
minority students by teaching them, as if these students had
not grown up in the real world, what the real world is like.

What if we thought of the university not as preparation
for a real and hostile world, but as the aspirational model
for a world where denigration would not be ubiquitous and
implicitly prioritized? Strossen's warnings about any type of
speech regulation setting us on a slippery slope is matched
by the liberal faith that listening to hate speech will turn
most listeners against hate. But there is scant evidence that
granting a platform to divisive and injurious speech by a

virulent racist, for instance, inevitably leads people to reject his or her ideas.

THE SLIPPERY SLOPE IS A MATTER OF FAITH

Floyd Abrams characterizes a Canadian high court's decision to prohibit speech demeaning the dignity of some people "thoughtful, sensitive, and powerful [but] flatly at odds with long-standing American jurisprudence." It turns out that the fear of a slippery slope is not based on concrete evidence, which cannot be measured, that the suppression of speech will always be a detriment. It is simply asserted, as a matter of faith, that the expansion of speech protection will move us inexorably toward more freedom, even if the protected speech advocates the abolition of freedom itself. Indeed, while the common but far from self-explanatory term "slippery slope" is sometimes erroneously thought to originate in the discipline of logic, I suspect that the expression finds its way into jurisprudence from the New Testament wherein God protects his followers from "slipping" on their path and warns in James 2:10: "whoever keeps the entire law, and yet stumbles [or slips] at one point, is guilty of breaking it all." Even if the religious undertone, that even the tiniest deviation will bring down the entire legal system, is never recognized, it turns out that free speech absolutists invoke the slippery slope not because they have evidence for its inevitability but because it is American to invoke it as an article of unquestioning faith, and it is American, as a matter of faith rather than reason, to believe in the slippery slope.

For the context of the university, the idea that any speech regulation will lead to disastrous results is almost always tied to the notion of "offensive" speech. Among the feared outcomes is that any speech regulation, such as not spending resources on unscientific speakers peddling obsolete ideas, will deprive minority students of the exposure to the kind of hatred and bigotry which they will encounter in the real world. Renowned scholars including Jeremy Waldron, Kimberlé Crenshaw, Richard Delgado, Mari Matsuda, Ian Haney López, Catharine MacKinnon, Emily Bernard, Stefan Bradley, and Charles Lawrence, in addition to other scholars and students who I interviewed on the subject over the years, do not share the view that exposure to virulent racism and misogyny builds character. The differences among their viewpoints notwithstanding, they largely agree that some speech can be "injurious," by which they mean speech that materially interferes with the social good of equal participation in the public. These legal arguments have generated extensive debate. They have proven difficult to agree on because any definition of "offensive" must remain vague. One person's offense may be another person's entertainment.

THE EQUALITY PRINCIPLE DOES NOT LEAD TO A SLIPPERY SLOPE

In the university, however, "offense" may not be the most useful category. I use a narrower gauge for speech in higher education, where the only type of speech that needs to be regulated is one that interferes with the students' ability to study and learn. Speech that crosses this line is speech that disputes the inherent equality of all students based on group belonging. The definition of equality is the incontrovertible baseline for educational participation and access. This standard is sufficiently specific to prevent setting us on a slippery slope toward willful censorship. If an administrator decides not to pay for the use of a legitimating college platform for a white supremacist, this does not open the door to future administrators punishing all forms of dissent. If a hypothetical future speaker, along the slippery slope which Eugene Volokh shows is not a legal principle, advocates the innate inferiority of individuals based on belonging to a legally protected group, such speech would materially undermine the educational project in the same way. The same standard would remain in place, which guarantees reasoned and robust debate in the name of advancing knowledge. However, if a student group later tries to ban a speaker whose political views they find offensive, but who does not claim any group's inherent inferiority, and invokes as precedent the university's decision not to grant the neo-Nazis access to the quad, they still would not have grounds for limiting such speech.

WHO DRAWS THE LINE?

Who are you to draw the line? This key question, which I have been asked by students, faculty colleagues, and commentators of my work, often with considerable passion, is as much pragmatic as philosophical. As in all human institutions, from the family and playground to the classroom and to parliament, the power to make decisions, to unlock the proverbial or actual doors, needs to be gathered in one or several persons who can decide on behalf of others. Ideally, the individuals who hold such decision-making power are accountable to the community, have been chosen through a fair and just process, and must operate in a system of checks and balances of governance. In universities, that role finally falls to faculty and administrators, who are, for good reason, almost always trained and experienced in the process of vetting ideas for inclusion in debate. They must temper their faith in the power of truth and reasoned debate to prevail against people who do not respect the truth, do not believe in debate, and do not accept the university's expertise in defining its mission as distinct from that of a public street.

I advanced through the ranks of the university, from my freshman year at Berkeley through college and graduate school to a tenured faculty position and, for a bit over a decade, a senior leadership role. Whatever authority I have held, at every instance of my participation in higher education, has been limited by the governance structure that includes faculty and students, and that is intended not only to serve these groups as individuals but also to advance a larger mission. It has also been checked by my awareness that I am obliged to act in a manner morally aligned with the university's overall mission and not simply with the force of institutional authority, and that others might propose better steps. Any decision-making power granted to an administrator is based on extensive training, experience, and trust, and even though I have been directly involved in speech disputes, I am not a legal scholar, nor a philosopher. With all due respect to those professions, I would not hand to the courts, legislators, journalists, professional philosophers, and law professors, who will likely choose their domain's approach rather than balancing students, faculty and staff interests from a comprehensive vantage point, the exclusive power of deciding what speech contributes to the university and which narrow band of speech materially interferes with it.

But the question of who can draw the line rests on another, more complicated assumption. It presupposes that no lines had ever been drawn, that speech flourished unfettered in the university's unregulated marketplace of ideas, that the status quo is the best of all possible settings which appeared without flawed human intervention. Who are *you* to draw the line, hides the question: who before and after you is to draw a line? Which is among the reasons why speech debates regularly involve a stand-off between senior white men, including journalists, hectoring African-American students for failing to appreciate the Constitution. The question of who can draw the line when a controversial speaker or the neo-Nazis arrive on campus, implies that no line had existed before this sudden regulation. It implies that everyone had always been able to participate equally in speech in the public forum where speech matters. This, even if only looking at enrollment numbers over time, is not the case. It might also imply that we want to keep things to how they were before the courageous students came along who want to ban the Nazis, to the time when white supremacy, racism and misogyny were either the unspoken order of the day or just odious distractions. Lines had been drawn even then. Universities are reflections of how society provides access, distributes resources, organizes opportunity, and bestows authority. They are as much training facilities for future employment as they are communities with shared goals.

The speech debates are so volatile because they indicate the evolving needs of a society in transformation, with members who had never been silenced and today claim their equal rights with persistence, courage, and force. They are a consequence, in part, to the salutary opening of American campuses and society to more people and their diverse voices. Students, staff, and faculty demand the right of equal participation that had been denied, if unsuccessfully, to various groups via earlier sets of rules, when mostly white men had drawn the lines. They are not politicizing a neutral space, but reminding us that the parameters of this space are already political. Today's debates are testimony to the fact that some of these lines must be redrawn. They serve as a reminder of the fact (which is not merely an opinion) that lines have always existed, as they do for all human interactions. As Americans, we have proven especially vigilant in drawing lines to include more people in public debates, and to redraw or erase the lines that had for a long time excluded especially women and minority citizens from public discourse. To pretend that no lines exist, that the truth will win out on merit, that facts speak for themselves rather than require their organization into a comprehensible account, and that the university does not have the authority to make accuracy and truthfulness matter, may be intellectually satisfying. It is even a position occasionally advanced by university leaders. But it is historically inaccurate and bears no relation to the lived reality in today's universities to state that meaningful speech happens, and that truth will be winnowed from falsehood like a horse shaking off flies, without someone drawing lines.

When people define the university's method as "reasoned" debate, "civil" dialogue, and "truth-seeking" discourse, they use those terms to *presuppose* certain unwritten rules and norms of behavior. To regulate speech which disputes some students' inherent capacity and right to participate in the university on equal terms does not mean prohibiting all manners of uncivil, disrespectful, and offensive speech. It simply makes obvious a rule, and draws a line, that others had drawn differently at earlier times before the university committed, and became legally compelled, to provide equal participation by the force of law.

Instead of pushing back against the deliberate representation of how speech operates in the university, some faculty members have acquiesced to a caricature of their campus stifled by political correctness. They have decided that instead of thinking through the university's ground rules, it is easier to let the pseudo-scientists speak occasionally, even at great financial cost and in a serious compromise of the university's commitment to equality. They mistakenly think that this means not drawing a line but that odious ideas will be debated in a self-governing forum where the truth will win out. It has been striking to me that faculty in the natural sciences frequently consider the speech controversies not to concern them directly when these spectacles aim at undermining the role of expertise and the notion of establishing the truth. Even if the natural and social sciences rely on different methods, as Richard Foley has shown, they share the practice of drawing lines that around settled ideas that do not warrant further debate. Since the students know that the university routinely regulates which ideas merit debate, to them the university's claim of drawing no line for speakers who deny some students' humanity, looks unprincipled. Which, indeed, it is.

Every university should aim to allow for the greatest amount of speech within the parameters of its mission, which is education and research with equal rights of participation. The spurious idea of the innate inferiority of some racial groups, or of women, is not one of those ideas. It can be excluded, without setting us on a slippery slope to censorship and tyranny, just like pre-Newtonian physics, or a theory of light-conducting ether, is excluded from science classes without ending all future research.

Universities must do a better job of explaining their gatekeeping function. They must also maintain internal control over their mission. This means embedding student invitations, just like the approval of rental contracts for its facilities, in a structure of academic decision-making. It means defending the inherent value of respect for the truth, of evidence-based and reasoned argument, and of free speech enjoyed, as political philosopher Hannah Arendt insisted as vital for a democracy, by diverse equals. It is worth recalling Arendt's explanation, in her 1963 essay "Truth and Politics," of why politically independent universities are crucial in a free society:

> Very unwelcome truths have emerged from the universities, and very unwelcome judgments have been handed down from the bench time and again; and these institutions, like other refuges of truth, have remained exposed to all the dangers arising from social and political power. Yet the chances for truth to prevail in public are, of course, greatly improved by the mere existence of such places and by the organization of independent, supposedly disinterested scholars associated with them. And it can hardly be denied that, at least in constitutionally ruled countries, the political realm has recognized, even in the event of conflict, that it has a stake in the existence of men and institutions over which it has no power.

The line, to be perfectly clear, should be drawn within the university with courage and conviction. Arendt would be horrified by legislative efforts and self-appointed watchdog groups to dictate what must be taught and debated in the university on political grounds. She draws a line around the organization of independent scholars who pursue the truth, not to serve a political agenda, but for its own sake. She also wanted the university to remain apolitical, and she overlooked how politicized it was already in her time. But the university is the place where many lines about speech and behavior already exist, as they do in all workplaces, and in the public institutions whose "political function of supplying information," in Arendt's hopeful words "is exercised from outside the political realm."

7

SPEECH ON CAMPUS

How It Can Work

IN THE FALL OF 2015 a rising senior at Yale University lost her temper for a moment and, raising her voice and using a common epithet, confronted a university administrator for what she perceived to be insensitive advice on how to deal with offensive Halloween costumes. Thanks to a cell phone video, the scene became a flash point in the current culture wars, pitting what a national magazine labeled a "coddled" generation of oversensitive students against reasonable adults. The testimony of the student's demand of not wanting to be demeaned, even if others defined it as bawdy humor or provocation, stood in conflict with the professor's faith in the power of dialogue and, many in the ensuing debate claimed, against "Reason" itself. Instead of giving the benefit of the doubt to the student's complaint about the institution which exists to educate people like her, commentators seized upon the 120-second video as evidence of a grave threat to free speech in America. In the courts of public opinion, similar protests, especially by students of color at many universities, have been criticized as threatening our country's hallowed tradition of free speech.

Free speech is in fact a narrow lens through which to understand what is at stake in the college debates. It is narrow because it imports a legal concept, which has changed throughout history, into a place where freedom of inquiry and robust debate are put in the service of exploring new ideas, learning, and advancing knowledge. What happened in this and similar scenes, such as protests in the fall of 2015 at the University of Missouri when students interpreted their school's response to racist incidents as the tacit condoning of discriminatory practices, left me wondering why so many commentators, including many professors tasked with educating the next generation, dismissed the students' complaints so harshly. Alumni were aghast, and saw the current generation's concerns as breaking with the ideals which they had fought for in their heyday as student activists. I was taken aback by the severity of the response. As a teacher and administrator, but also as a parent and an American, I consider it my responsibility to listen attentively to the next generation. When a student says that something is not right in my classroom or institution, my first impulse is to find out more and not to shut down the complaint. To listen closely to someone whose education has been entrusted to me is as much a moral as an professional obligation. More broadly, it is every educator's task to discern what does not work for those growing up in our country and institutions, and to accept that the next generation may use means of expression unfamiliar to older generations. The students' complaints may be angry, righteous, and impatient. But such expressions are characteristic of the young. In the case of the protests over speech, they also claim an indisputable authority vested in their identity. And here the true conflict seems to begin.

It is an apparently irreconcilable conflict between experience, rooted in personal subjectivity, on the one side, and argument and the authority of abstract, objective reasoning, on the other. On the one hand, we have a student's righteous outburst staked on personal identity against what she sees as her institution's condoning or downplaying as thoughtless jokes and pranks the practices that have long prevented students from properly learning. The outburst was directed at professors and administrators, but it is really aimed at the institution itself. On the other side, we have a professionally accredited but momentarily defensive adult appealing to the structure, culture, and tradition of reasoned argument, civil dialogue, and robust debate. The student cites the right to participate in the university on equal terms as a fundamental moral and legal value. The faculty cites unfettered debate, where everyone can voice any opinion, as the university's fundamental value. Both sides, as do other students and faculty caught up in these issues, claim that they have been gravely wronged. Can they be reconciled?

SPEAKING "MY" TRUTH

The students speak from a place of experience. Their truth is the cultural, political, and legal validation, or, in some situations, the denigration of their personhood, or identity, as members of the university community who may constitute a numerical minority but are there as rightfully as any other person. They also call on the university's commitment to act on its values, which include equality. The university administrator and the loud chorus of commentators speak from a place that they define as the place of reason itself. They also occupy a position of power in the university, which is an institution that plays a critical role in society by providing access and opportunities, and by legitimating certain types of knowledge and debate over others. Instead of citing the value of equality, they insist that presenting as many viewpoints as possible, including offensive or racist ones, is a benefit for all. How can we hope to reconcile the authority of subjective experience with the authority of reasoned argument? Is it not the university's purpose to teach and practice the use of reason as a method to overcome subjective, parochial, and emotional concerns and opinions, and is absolutely unfettered debate not the best way to heal a world splintering into competing factions? Hannah Arendt considered it the paramount task of politics to balance the Socratic method of enabling each individual to access his or her truth with the Platonic wish for an absolute truth that applies to all humans in the same way. She cautioned against a "tyranny of the truth" found in Plato's polemic against personal opinion, which is the mode in which a truth becomes available to many in the public, but was also sympathetic to the need for a higher authority in a world that would otherwise, without any such anchoring principles, become rooted in myriad personal opinions, and become inhuman.

If students claim unassailable authority based on the absolute primacy of "their" truth, which is close to what Plato condemned as mere opinion (which we could call "subjective"), don't we just end up with a hopeless struggle over whose experience matters most? And, critically, shouldn't the university stay out of disputes over offended feelings and inflamed passions and let students, faculty, and the invited speaker hash this out for themselves, except when it leads to violence or other destructive behavior? What would be a world in which everyone's experience and identity matters to such a degree that no broader way of thinking, in the form of an appeal to our shared humanity, justice, or fundamental rights such as free speech, or any other lasting principles, such as reason and truth, has the authority to define all of us in shared terms? The inevitable outcome of any self-understanding that includes particular identities, many people think, is the dissolution of our social bonds, which rest on collectively shared values that respect but do not prioritize difference.

WE DO NOT HAVE TO CHOOSE BETWEEN FREE SPEECH AND EQUALITY

The students point out, and I have argued in this book by drawing on a range of thinkers from law and philosophy and on in-depth structured conversations with dozens of faculty and students, in addition to over two decades of teaching and working in university administration, that a doctrinaire notion of free speech is used to exclude some groups from the educational setting rather than to expand the possibility of robust debate. Their protests may strike many as overwrought and dangerously close to unacceptable censorship. But their concerns are echoed in the highest echelons of the legal profession. Legal scholars such as Robert Post, Julie Suk, Richard Delgado, Fred Schauer, Stanley Fish, and Kimberlé Crenshaw worry about a blanket application of First Amendment absolutism, or a kind of First Amendment "opportunism," at the expense of other rights, even if they do not agree at all on the appropriateness of the student protests.

The students do not believe that identity is a newfangled conception which has destroyed politics, but that the identity of powerful groups has long been inscribed in only nominally neutral principles at the expense of equality. They do not believe that when women and minority students demand equal treatment, this demand replaces fair policies with obsessive self-absorption. Instead, their critique underscores that when white men govern out of self-interest, their identity is frequently established as normative, worthy and superior to others. They occasionally also claim that the very definition of the primacy of reason, open debate, and even freedom of speech, in its conventional guise, oppresses their voices and identities. This has led to difficult scenes, when students have critiqued syllabi as inherently discriminatory and shown little willingness to accept other points of view. The students want to dis-identify with the demand to assume a fixed identity, but often do so while turning their assigned but soon-to-be-discarded identity into a badge of moral authority. Often, though, when students demand that the university ensure an equal educational setting, the response is that they should have faith in the university's elegant ability to host speakers whose views the institution condemns. They are told that speech *about* inferiority, just "ideas," is very different from the imposition of inferiority by an invited speaker. They are told to have faith that the university upholds equality, while hosting speakers who dispute the value of doing so. They are told, by a chorus of journalists and academics, that their speech is a threat to liberal politics, and that they should fall back in line until their issues can be addressed with all deliberate speed. They are told that the rules of open debate are fair for all participants, since the only limit is on speech that incites immediate violence.

The students, however, along with some faculty, do not think that only direct incitement to immediate violence interferes with their right to participate on equal terms in the community of learners. Who are they to define such speech?, intones a chorus of critics. What if one person's offense is another person's reasonable idea? But no reasonable person should be in doubt about speakers whose established message is to advocate an ethno-state, the inherent inferiority and criminality of minority groups, or the notion that women should be excluded from certain tasks because of innate inferiority. Such speech, when the speaker is on record as proposing chiefly such views, is an expressive means of imposing inequality, both in the immediate context of the event and in the institution. It flourishes on the internet, where people participate not as fully embodied citizens but with varying degrees of anonymity and lesser degrees of accountability than in direct encounters. But in a university, there is a compelling interest to prevent such an expressive practice of inequality, which effectively, and impermissibly, singles out students, teachers, or staff members of particular backgrounds. By inviting such speakers, the university does not remain neutral but in fact takes action against its educational mission and the principle of equality which it must uphold.

In these cases, many commentators think they must choose between speech rights and equality. I do not believe that this is the right choice. Differently put, I believe that pitting individual liberty against equality, rather than viewing equality, liberty, and dignity as equally important and interdependent, and examining how each concept comes with different histories and political weight, stacks the debate in ways that bypass the university's concerns. Universities can and must uphold the ground rules of equal participation in the educational enterprise. These rules must be based exclusively on merit and not group characteristics, without punishing anyone's speech. Such rules must be flexible enough to allow for a vast range of differing opinions, including controversial and, yes, even deeply offensive ones. Having ground rules does not mean instituting speech codes, legislating civility, or restricting debate. Historian Joan Scott has cautioned against reflexively invoking civility, which can become a moralistic type of ground rule, as a means of limiting necessary debate. Scott cites the university's prerogative of deploying academic expertise to advance "the common good," which excludes some types of information even when very defined in the most capacious terms. This "common good," I believe, must be staked on equality and liberty in order to be meaningful. When universities are admonished to adhere to a rigid conception of absolute speech rights that compromises the equality principle, this elevation of speech over the student's right to participate in debate on equal terms renders the practice of unfettered debate at the heart of higher education all but meaningless.

THE LANGUAGE OF ARGUMENT VERSUS THE LANGUAGE OF FORCE

I believe that our Founders' principles of freedom and equality are worth the strongest possible defense. I also believe that these principles remain revolutionary in the sense that they can be achieved for all. I think that robust debate—including engaging with views you may consider deeply upsetting—is our path forward. I just do not believe that reason and debate are self-governing processes that can work without ground rules. Reason, as a category, means, in practice, the giving of reasons. They are never only the reasons given by God, Aristotle, Plato, or Immanuel Kant, nor by Thomas Jefferson, Frederick Douglass, the Supreme Court, a university president, Hannah Arendt, or any legislator. Reason means the historical give and take by practitioners who accept and revise the rules as diverse equals. But not all speakers want to allow for ground rules that allow everyone to speak. Some speech deliberately aims to invalidate our respect for reason, and instead appeals directly to unreason and emotion, or functions in other ways to exclude people from debate. While our courts have placed even "factual error and defamatory content" under constitutional protection, in a case decided in 1964, in the university such blanket protections conflict with the university's mission, which the courts have also recognized as worthy of protection. The university's purpose is to replace such authoritative language, which operates as force and can be the language of the state but also of public opinion, in the form of the tyranny of the majority, or an impassioned online mob, with the language of argument. This is a lofty and honorable goal. For it to be realized, universities must retain their right to recognize that not all speech accepts the rules of argument. Some types of speech, including extremist racist speech, does not depend on and therefore cannot be defeated with reason. Such speech seeks legitimation but not consensus, because it seeks to exclude some people a priori from participating in the battle to reach agreement. In the university, where speech serves the specific purposes of education and research in pursuit of the truth, authoritative speech counters the very mission of the institution to turn this type of argument rather than force into a standard for the acceptance of ideas.

Speech that refuses to accept the primacy of reason and advocates fundamental inequality enjoys remarkable support in our vibrant democracy. I leave open, instead of clearly siding with Plato here, whether it genuinely contributes to the well-being of our country. I harbor serious doubts whether the protection of such speech (which the Supreme Court acknowledged but has not addressed further as a core constitutional issue in a 1952 case, *Beauharnais v. Illinois*, of fascist group libel against Black Americans), is truly the single indispensable safeguard for our democracy to survive, as many speech absolutists maintain. Although it is not often cited as precedent in subsequent cases dealing with similar issues, the Supreme Court has never explicitly overturned its ruling in *Beauharnais*. But our country has evolved. This evolution has resulted not only in a surging populist movement staked on identity politics while attacking minorities, but also in a more diverse population of students, which means that in many institutions there is no longer a numerical majority of one demographic group. This is why universities serve as the testing ground for our nation's consensus, as Danielle Allen underlines, that *all* Americans should enjoy equal rights in a robust democracy, including the individual right to free expression, and not only those who had benefitted from rules made only for them.

THE UNIVERSITY AS A TEST CASE FOR DEMOCRACY

Even in their revolutionary optimism, our nation's Founders probably did not envision universities where men and women of diverse backgrounds would converge to pursue the highest calling for any human being, which is to improve oneself in order to improve the greater good. It's instructive to picture Jefferson or Madison strolling across the quad of one of today's major public institutions amidst the diversity of students committed to improving themselves. Jefferson, of course, thought "that every citizen in [our country] should receive an education proportioned to the condition and pursuits of his life." Today, when all Americans are granted the right to pursue a life without such constraints, education is all the more important. Even if the Founders could not imagine today's diverse students, they ignited a radical vision, adumbrated powerfully by the likes of Frederick Douglass and countless women activists, with their claim of non-negotiable equality. The "we" which had once been limited in scope has progressed to include ever more people and inspired generations of Americans, including citizens of color and women, even when they had been deprived of fundamental rights, to exercise what Jefferson called "unalienable rights" *without* explicit governmental protection. The great tradition of free speech includes previously excluded groups who claimed this right in the true sense of the term not by invoking a legal principle but by speaking out without formal legitimation. They opposed the long-standing and wrong-headed practice of turning constitutional law against them, and of turning free speech into a weapon to dismantle disfavored policies.

Their speech transformed the history of our country as an event, in the sense of an occurrence that transforms the conditions under which it occurs. Free speech became a reality in this nation not when the Court decided for it to be so, but when courageous individuals spoke out for freedom and equality, and when poets and artists seized a right to free expression, *in spite of* the law not applying to them.

THE COURAGE OF SNOWFLAKES

Today's students, like all younger generations, also exercise their right to speak without waiting for permission. They have little patience for speakers who dredge up disproven racial theories about the innate inferiority of some, or who invoke free speech rights while disregarding and disrespecting the framework of such rights in general, which include not lying under oath, or cloaking an agenda of violence in the garb of expression. And they wonder why such speech, which revives ideas long laid to rest by a consensus of experts, is given preferential treatment and sponsored at enormous cost, while the university excludes all sorts of other obsolete ideas on a daily basis. Instead of applauding the students' courage to speak out when someone tries to take that right away by making them prove their humanity, liberals and conservatives have dismissed the students as coddled, hyper-sensitive, and irrational "snowflakes." This scornful vocabulary, laced with anger and contempt, hews close to the timeless tactics used to silence minorities and women who critique their unequal treatment, describing them as overly emotional, shrill, manipulative, and dishonest. There has been handwringing over the younger generation's increasing unwillingness to bestow the university's prestige and resources on speech that claims some humans are innately inferior and therefore do not deserve equal treatment before the law, or the right to exist in our country, in the university, or anywhere at all. In my conversations with students, they have proven sharply discerning about how to improve today's universities lest it harbor some remnant of the odious parts of Jefferson's worldview. But the students are not sacrificing our country's

Aristotle already spotted in the youth of his era, but whose viewpoint I consider, as Aristotle had done, worth examining.

The anger might originate from a sense of loss when a worldview is challenged and some comforting or empowering ideas, which are part of the status quo, are in the process of being rendered obsolete for good. Among these ideas are the notions that some races are innately inferior, or at least have yet to prove their full equality, and that women, in their difference from men, are naturally unfit for equal rights. There is also the spectacle of a generation of aging campus activists who feel that their legacy is threatened and who have been duped by the narrative, which kept them in the role of radicals and heroes, that today's racist firebrands carry the mantle of Mario Savio who started the Free Speech Movement in Berkeley. But there is another, more timely reason. The anxiety produced by speech issues on campus surely also results from the understandable reflex to defend freedom of expression at a moment when the American president flouts respect for the truth, systematically attacks and threatens the press, and ignores the decorum of respectfully disagreeing with, rather than disparaging, politicians, journalists, or regular citizens. The highest officers in our government deny and reject scientific consensus. In response, people resort to the idea of absolute speech rights because they fear that the right to speak their mind, which everyone experiences on a personal and visceral level, may be at risk even in the United States. What had seemed like an abstract if complicated principle, in light of a global surge of populism, seems threatened by a government that routinely disparages the press, does not believe in science, and denies the existence of proven facts. If politicians had always played fast and loose with the truth especially during elections, scholars such as

Ruth Ben-Ghiat and Jason Stanley have pointed out, our current government now directly disparages expert opinion and elevates falsehood to a new level for the sake of disorienting the public and redefining the terms of public discourse. This new situation blinds commentators to the fact that universities have been baited into a deliberately distorted debate. Understandably worried about their own speech rights, and about the freedom of the press, they are not conducting the debate over campus speech in intellectually honest ways.

It is disconcerting to witness eminent scholars and journalists berate the students for failing to appreciate that the First Amendment was always on the side of the powerless. It is also understandable. But even a cursory review of our country's jurisprudence proves that the story is more complicated. But the scholars hope to encourage the students to uphold our nation's principles at a moment when the unwritten norms of democratic behavior, which include civil debate, cannot be taken for granted. Instead of declaring that our country's definition of speech has been stable and unchanging through history, which is not accurate, these scholars could lead us out of the current impasse by disentangling the deliberate confusion of the notions of free speech, freedom of the press, and freedom of academic inquiry. Legal scholars can help by drawing attention, not only in the rarefied halls of law schools and the erudite pages of academic journals but through public media, to the difference between a university and the public sphere, instead of lumping various issues under First Amendment principles that do not apply in the same way in all contexts. The specific context of the university is a productive place to test our nation's commitments to both equality and free speech. At this moment, we do well to note that the students alert us to what courts ought to defend: a vibrant democracy without governmental suppression of opposing viewpoints.

The current campus flare-ups remind us that work remains to be done in our country's bold transformation to achieve a reality where all Americans enjoy the greatest amount of personal liberty. This work means being honest and truthful about how free speech has worked historically. It requires not clinging to a rigid notion of speech rights that travel through all contexts, work the same everywhere, and trump all other principles. A vast library of legal reflection on the matter and our courts' fascinatingly varied definitions of speech throughout time suggests that such a rigid notion is of little use in real-world settings. Speech rights must be defined carefully to make them a lived reality for as many Americans as possible today. Universities ought to be in the vanguard of this work, since it is their function, in both teaching and research, to assess the utility and value of different kinds of speech. They need to do a better job of explaining how they distinguish between ideas that merit debate, and how efforts to sever the concept of free speech from its roots in equality undermines the principles of education. They ought to get back in the business of not only creating knowledge but, especially when it comes to the next generation, of showing moreal leadership and of providing hope.

The argument that free speech rests securely and always on the side of reason and moral progress is well-intentioned but regrettably inaccurate. When students protest speech on campus and are told to back off, or threatened with penalties, because free speech alone, as an abstract principle, will ensure moral progress and bring forth the truth, the fact that speech rights had to *become* a force for good is overlooked.

But in the university, we have an obligation, at the heart of genuine teaching, to enable the next generation to be heard.

Teaching and governing does not only require experience, knowledge, and wisdom. It means activating another's capacity for independent thinking, and transforming what a student says, which is as often based on intuition as on knowledge, into something that makes sense to others in general terms. Teaching means not only imparting accurate information but providing the next generation with the proper means of expression, which might lie outside the existing paradigms of acceptable speech. Thinking, which lies at the heart of teaching, is difficult. You don't just know how to do it, just like you cannot just run onto a football field or cricket pitch, assume the right positions, and play. Thinking, as the mind's capacity to hold several thoughts at once and assess their respective and interdependent validity, can and must be learned; it is a skill that can be acquired. When Simone Weil was asked to provide guidelines on how to rebuild French society after the Nazi occupation during World War II, she wrote: "Nothing . . . is more frightful than to see some poor wretch in the police court stammering before a magistrate who keeps up an eloquent flow of witticisms." What Weil found morally upsetting was not the stammering wretch but the magistrate who wielded his eloquence and learning as a weapon. The witticisms produced by writers and pundits who label students "snowflakes," "coddled," "overly sensitive," "excellent sheep," "entitled," and "not ready for the real world" have one underlying note: condescension. Weil considered this sentiment an especially grave failure for anyone with authority. For such people, condescension can quickly turn into the inappropriate use of the force they have been granted by an institution. I think our nation's students are not poor wretches pleading to a magistrate, whether in the figures of senior scholars, journalists, pundits, and the president, all of whom regularly belittle and dismiss them, to shelter them from challenges. They are tremendously courageous in carrying on, in excelling in study and research, and in claiming their right not to be placed in a position to defend their existence, or the existence of their peers.

After Charlottesville, when the Nazis' and Klan's reliance on free speech was exposed as a ruse to drive minorities from the public sphere, the battle cry of absolute speech rights, which had never been recognized by the law, looks ill-considered. For minority populations in this country, who continue to be over-policed even in elite universities, the threat is real. To claim that free speech is distributed evenly on many sides, meaning that students who complain are treated in the same way as non-university guests who dispute some students' right to exist in our nation, is a misleading instance of moral relativism. Americans fear that any restriction on speech will lead to fascism. After Virginia, and in a period when our democratic institutions are being put to an unprecedented test, Americans may also fear, as Europeans and Canadians do, that completely unfettered speech can damage our democracy.

The students' methods can be counterproductive or even destructive, and in some instances they do not leave a lot of room for goodwill on many listeners' parts. The problem is that for any political results to happen, there has to be consensus or compromise, yet the demands of students do not always allow for that. It is the responsibility of teachers or administrators to pay close attention. We may not like what we hear. We may be unfamiliar with or dislike the way things are expressed. But the students are saying that something is not working. To shut down their complaint with an overly abstract conception of free speech is an abdication of our responsibilities. We are not obligated to give the students immediate credence at face value. We also do not have to let the claim of their experience take absolute priority over reason or argument, or overlook that their claims are often based on reason, too. But we need to work with them on what rules constitute reasoned debate so they can participate fully in the university.

By invoking personal experience as unquestionable truth, the students rely on a shift in our culture over the past 50 years that harks back to Enlightenment principles. The idea that every individual human being on the planet matters inherently, and that every person has a right to tell his or her version of events from his or her perspective, is a relatively recent concept. It originates in the Enlightenment idea that every citizen matters equally, formulated at the time when top-down monarchic rule changed to republican governance in some places, and of which our country is an exceptional example. Today, the notion is more accepted that every single person matters and has the right to speak for him or herself. This idea of every human being's equal worth was first conceived as a political concept at the historical moment when freedom, equality, and also freedom of speech were enshrined in our Constitution and its Amendments. It is the radical idea at the heart of America, which the students are activating in the name of equality and freedom.

The issue is not one of deciding whether the privileging of experience over argument is good or bad. An irreversible shift has taken place. On the positive side, the fact that people can testify to their experience which is heard and believed has dislodged unequal social arrangements. The Black Lives

Matter and #MeToo movements are examples of this shift, and it is not clear how the tension between personal experience, now amplified thanks to the courageous organizing by individuals such as Tarana Burke, and a system designed to silence those experiences, and sometimes reward that silence, will be resolved. It is no longer only the powerful that matter, but also those who had been excluded. These new stories expose that "reason" had been defined in ways that privilege some accounts over others. Personal testimony to one's identity can, for activists of *all* political stripes, invalidate collective consensus.

What to do at this impasse? In order to find common ground between the generations, university administrators need to recall that their primary role is not to be abstract philosophers or First Amendment experts. They have a clear responsibility to define what speech must be included in the shared enterprise of free inquiry, and which ideas do not merit debate for the reasons I outline in this book. Instead of citing a disembodied conception of absolute speech rights, which is not found in American jurisprudence, universities ought to uphold the compelling interests of education, which means not forcing some students, faculty, and staff into defending their humanity while others simply do their work. The issue is one of equality, not limiting offense. There must not be incommensurate and impossible requirements placed on some members of the university whose humanity is put into question. In addition to undermining the equality of the educational setting, such claims can lead only to unconstitutional actions which are violent, morally bankrupt, and scientifically obsolete.

University administrators owe it to the public to explain the procedures by which faculty decide on a daily basis which ideas receive a hearing and which create enabling conditions for speech to foster new knowledge and, importantly, *hope*. Universities must not abdicate their responsibility to make difficult decisions and leave them exclusively to student groups, legislators, and outsiders, just as faculty cannot allow just anyone to dictate what should be taught in a classroom. While the process of arriving at a scholarly consensus differs between the social and the natural sciences, as Richard Foley has explained, science faculty should articulate their principles for vetting invited speakers and excluding some speech routinely to underline the university's overarching mission and acknowledge the threat posed by speech controversies to academic mechanisms of establishing a truth. Institutions must create mechanisms to balance the many interests in their community, in order not to restrict speech but to adhere to our nation's laws in allowing everyone to take part in the exchange of ideas on equal terms. They must correct the caricature of a university threatened by political correctness and fragile students, and fight back against a hollow conception of free speech that owes nothing to First Amendment jurisprudence but is aimed at ending the equality in higher education that was legally mandated 50 years ago, and the culture of respecting reasoned argument as a way of establishing the truth. They must institute policies and deploy resources to make true on the value of equality, and not only speak about it. The point is not to turn university administrators into philosopher-kings who decide between useful and useless political ideas in the public arena, and, as Plato had advocated in his great worry over the power of public opinion after the trial of Socrates, who have the power to arbitrate between mere opinion and a universal truth. But university faculty and administrators should be able and indeed authorized to decide what the university is. In some cases, this means excluding from academic debate ideas that exist in the realm of public opinion but do not further and indeed undermine learning and research.

Student organizations must also abide by the university's methods of vetting ideas based on expertise, and learn how scarce resources are allocated not to grant outsiders free publicity but to advance understanding, further reasoned debate, and ensure equal participation of all. They need to learn that by not inviting every speaker to the stage of a university with limited resources, nobody has been punished. In my view, these debates will be more productive when framed as issues of equality and not matters of personal offense.

Journalists may want to step back before asserting the tempting but false equivalence of freedom of the press and freedom of speech *on campus*. Pundits should spend more time listening to students rather than rehashing the tired tropes of a culture war. By defending absolute, meaning unrestricted rights for anyone to speak on campus, journalists claim a privilege their editors deny to nearly all aspiring opinion-writers. The agitators and media personalities who yearn for the prestige, legitimation, and publicity of the university, in fact want to wrest the vetting power over what ideas qualify for debate from both the media and universities. They want to bring back ideas which have been discredited in our country but survive in the public sphere, where they thrive largely unregulated on social media platforms. Sometimes this happens for purposes of reconsidering obsolete ideas, and not to argue for the kind of inequality our country rejected, as a principle if not a practice, at the moment of its founding. Our country's courts should staunchly protect every citizen's right to express such ideas there. But self-appointed free-speech absolutists should spend less time berating university students for forsaking the First Amendment, and more time explaining how our country's speech protections have changed over time to truly protect everyone's freedoms, and how the university is a different place from the public at large. They should not demand special rights on campus for those claiming some people's inherent inferiority, rights which would not be automatically granted in many of their own publications or platforms. Our impulse should be to use and invoke the law to advance freedom and equality, rather than rely on it rigidly, and against the spirit and intentions of the Founders, to protect a status quo that does not yet fully realize America's great promise. It would be refreshing, and it strikes me as profoundly American, to see as fervent a defense of the Fourteenth Amendment, which enshrines in solemn law our democracy's bedrock principle of equality, as we routinely witness an often rigid and absolutist defense of the equally important First Amendment. Supreme Court rulings often structure public discussion, but the spirit of the law to secure our freedom depends on a historical and politically informed understanding of actual society to unfold beyond the judicious confines of particular rulings.

The university can create enabling conditions for speech without compromising the constitutional protections afforded each citizen from government suppression. It will take moral courage to so. But in the university where equality is not merely a concept subordinated to individual interests but a necessary condition, and where advancing knowledge is an academic rather than political activity, ideas that claim people's inherent inferiority will not get the privileged hearing their proponents demand. Such ideas will be studied as sociological artifacts from a past this country has officially left behind. If our government were to equivocate on the self-evident truth that all men are created equal, universities, and also artists, playwrights, filmmakers, writers and poets play an ever more important role to mark such ideas as not deserving of debate.

BIBLIOGRAPHY

Abdelarahman, Salma. "How should a university deal with its past complicities with slavery and pseudo-scientific racism." Interview on *Think About It*, www.ulrichbaer.com, October 8, 2018.

Abrams, Floyd. *The Soul of the First Amendment*. New Haven, CT: Yale University Press, 2016.

Allen, Danielle. *Education and Equality*. Chicago: University of Chicago Press, 2016.

Amar, Akhil Reed. *America's Unwritten Constitution*. New York: Basic Books, 2012.

American Academy of Arts and Sciences. *Introducing the Humanities Indicators: An Online Prototype of National Data Collection in the Humanities*. Cambridge, MA: American Academy of Arts and Sciences, 2009.

Arendt, Hannah. *Crises of the Republic*. New York: Penguin Press, 1973.

Arendt, Hannah. *The Human Condition*. Chicago: University of Chicago Press, 1958.

Arendt, Hannah. "On Truth in Politics." Originally published in *The New Yorker*, February 25, 1967, and reprinted with minor changes in *Between Past and Future*, New York: Penguin, 1968.

Aristotle. *Poetics*. New York: Penguin, 2012.

Ash, Timothy Garton. *Free Speech. Ten Principles for a Connected World.* New Haven, CT: Yale University Press, 2017.

Aurelius, Marcus. *Meditations.* New York: Dover Editions, 2015.

Baer, Ulrich. *Think About It* (podcast). www.ulrichbaer.com. Initial release date October 8, 2018.

Bejan, Teresa. *Mere Civility: Disagreement and the Limits of Toleration.* Cambridge, MA: Harvard University Press, 2017.

Ben-Ghiat, Ruth. "Trump's 'Trial Balloons' Test our Commitment to Freedom." *CNN* Opinion, November 8, 2017.

Ben-Porath, Sigal. *Free Speech on Campus.* Philadelphia: University of Pennsylvania Press, 2017.

Bilgrami, Akeel and Jonathan Cole, eds. *Who's Afraid of Academic Freedom.* New York: Columbia University Press, 2016.

Bok, Derek, and William G. Bowen. *The Shape of the River.* Princeton, NJ: Princeton University Press, 2000.

Bollinger, Lee. *The Tolerant Society.* New York and Oxford: Oxford University Press, 1988.

Bowen, William, and Michael McPherson. *Lesson Plan: An Agenda for Change in American Higher Education.* Princeton, NJ: Princeton University Press, 2015.

Bradley, Stefan. *Upending the Ivory Tower: Civil Rights, Black Power and the Ivy League.* New York: New York University Press, 2018.

Brooks, David. "How to Engage a Fanatic." *The New York Times,* October 3, 2017.

Carter, Prudence. Interview. *Think About It* Podcast. August 29, 2018.

Chemerinsky, Erwin, and Howard Gillman. *Free Speech on Campus.* New Haven, CT: Yale University Press, 2017.

Chemerinsky, cited in "The Free Speech/Hate Speech Trade-Off," in *The New York Times,* September 13, 2017.

Chemerinsky, Erwin. *The Case Against the Supreme Court.* New York: Penguin, 2015.

Christ, Carol. "Free Speech Is Who We Are." *Berkeley News,* August 23, 2017.

Cohen, Robert, and Reginald Zelnik, eds. *The Free Speech Movement: Reflections on Berkeley in the 1960s.* Berkeley: University of California Press, 2002.

Cole, David. "Why Free Speech Is Not Enough." *New York Review of Books*, March 23, 2017.

Cole, David. "Why We Must Still Defend Free Speech." *New York Review of Books*, December 28, 2017.

Crenshaw, Kimberlé, with Charles Lawrence, Richard Delgado, and Mary Matsuda. *Words That Wound: Critical Race Theory, Assaultive Speech and the First Amendment.* New York: Westview Press, 1993.

Darwin, Charles. *The Descent of Man.* New York: Prometheus, 1997.

de Tocqueville, A. *Democracy in America.* New York: Vintage Classics 1990 [1835–1840].

Delgado, Richard, and Jean Stefancic. *Must We Defend Nazis? Why the First Amendment Should Not Protect Hate Speech and White Supremacy.* New York: New York University Press, 2018.

Deresiewicz, William. *Excellent Sheep: The Miseducation of the American Elite and the Way to a Meaningful Life.* New York: Free Press, 2014.

Dewey, John. *Democracy and Education.* New York: Free Press, 1916.

Dewey, John. "My Pedagogic Creed." *The School Journal* 54, no. 3 (1897): 77–80.

Douglass, Frederick. *Autobiographies: Narrative of the Life of Frederick Douglass, an American Slave / My Bondage and My Freedom / Life and Times of Frederick Douglass.* New York: Library of Congress, 1994.

DuBois, W. E. B. *The Souls of Black Folk.* New York: Library of America, 1903.

Fish, Stanley. *The First.* Unpublished manuscript, 2018.

Fish, Stanley. *There Is No Such Thing as Free Speech, and It's a Good Thing, Too.* Oxford: Oxford University Press, 1994.

Foley, Richard. *The Geography of Insight: The Sciences, the Humanities, How They Differ, Why They Matter.* New York: Oxford University Press, 2018.

Foucault, Michel. *Fearless Speech.* Cambridge, MA: Semiotext(e), 2001.

Fouche-Channer, Addis. "Interview." Introduction and interview by Clara Wilson-Hawken. In *Re-Imagining a Safe Space.* NYU

Tisch Department of Photography and Imagining, October 26, 2017.

Franklin, Benjamin. "On Freedom of Speech and the Press," in *The Complete Works of Benjamin Franklin: Including His Private as Well as His Official and Scientific Correspondence.* New York: Forgotten Books, 2018.

French, David. "It's Time to Crush Campus Censorship," in *National Review*, April 27, 2017.

George, Robert, and Cornel West. *Truth Seeking, Democracy, and Freedom of Thought and Expression - A Statement by Robert P. George and Cornel West.* Princeton University, James Madison Program, March 2017.

Gould, Stephen Jay. *The Mismeasure of Man.* New York: Norton, 1996.

Gunier, Lani. *The Tyranny of the Meritocracy: Democratizing Higher Education in America.* Boston: Beacon Press, 2013.

Gutmann, Amy. *Identity in Democracy.* Princeton, NJ: Princeton University Press, 2003.

Jaspers, Karl. *The Idea of the University.* Boston: Beacon Press, 1959.

Jefferson, Thomas. "A Bill of the More General Diffusion of Knowledge," in *The Papers of Thomas Jefferson*, Volume 2. Princeton, NJ: Princeton University Press, 2017.

Kahlenberg, D., ed. *The Future of Affirmative Action: New Paths to Higher Education Diversity After* Fisher v. University of Texas. Washington, DC: Century Foundation, 2013.

Kalven, Harry. *The Negro and the First Amendment.* Columbus: Ohio State University Press, 1965.

Kenny, Sarah. "A Student's Perspective on Charlottesville." Interview on *Think About It*, www.ulrichbaer.com, October 8, 2018.

Keohane, Nannerl. *Thinking About Leadership.* Princeton, NJ: Princeton University Press, 2010.

Kerr, Clark. *The Uses of the University.* Cambridge, MA: Harvard University Press, 2001.

Kitcher, Philip. *Science, Truth, and Democracy.* Oxford: Oxford University Press, 2001.

Kuhn, Thomas. *The Structure of Scientific Revolutions.* Chicago: The University of Chicago Press, 2012.

López, Ian Haney. *Dog Whistle Politics*. Oxford and New York: Oxford University Press, 2015.

Lyotard, Jean-François. *The Postmodern Condition. A Report on Knowledge*. Minneapolis: University of Minnesota Press, 1984.

MacKinnon, Catharine. *Only Words*. Cambridge, MA: Harvard University Press, 1995.

Madison, James, and Alexander Hamilton. *Federalist Papers*. New York: Dover, 2009.

Manne, Kate. *Down Girl: The Logic of Misogyny*. New York: Oxford University Press, 2018.

Martinez, Luna. "Speech in the University." Interview on *Think About It*, www.ulrichbaer.com, October 8, 2018.

Matsuda, Mary. *Where Is Your Body?: And Other Essays on Race, Gender, and the Law*. Boston: Beacon Press, 1997.

McPherson, M., and H. Brighouse, eds. *The Aims of Higher Education: Problems of Morality and Justice*. Chicago: University of Chicago Press, 2015.

Menand, Louis. *The Marketplace of Ideas: Reform and Resistance in the American University*. New York: Norton, 2015.

Mill, John Stuart. *The Basic Writings of John Stuart Mill: On Liberty, the Subjection of Women and Utilitarianism*. New York: Random House, 2015.

Nichols, Tom. *The Death of Expertise: The Campaign Against Established Knowledge and Why It Matters*. New York: Oxford University Press, 2017.

Nussbaum, Martha. *Not for Profit: Why Democracy Needs the Humanities*. Princeton, NJ: Princeton University Press, 2010.

Okeke, Cameron. "I'm a black UChicago graduate. Safe spaces got me through college." *Vox*, August 29, 2016.

Pelican, Jaroslav. *The Idea of the University: A Reexamination*. New Haven, CT: Yale University Press, 2003.

Plato. *The Republic*. New York: Penguin, 2007.

Post, Robert. *Democracy, Expertise, and Academic Freedom: A First Amendment Jurisprudence of the Modern State*. New Haven, CT: Yale University Press, 2013.

Rorty, Richard. *Achieving Our Country*. Cambridge, MA: Harvard University Press, 1996.

Roth, Michael. *Beyond the University. Why Liberal Education Matters.* New Haven, CT: Yale University Press, 2014.

Rousseau, Jean-Jacques. *The Social Contract and The First and Second Discourses.* Oxford and New York: Oxford University Press, 2002.

Schauer, Fred. *The Force of Law.* Cambridge, MA: Harvard University Press, 2015.

Scott, Joan. "How the Right Weaponized Free Speech." *Chronicle of Higher Education,* January 7, 2018.

Scott, Joan. "In the Age of Trump, a Chilling Atmosphere." Interview with Bill Moyers. October 2017. On billmoyers.com.

Scott, Joan. *Knowledge, Power, and Academic Freedom.* New York: Columbia University Press, 2019 (forthcoming).

Shklar, Judith. *American Citizenship: The Quest for Inclusion.* Cambridge, MA: Harvard University Press, 1989.

Stanley, Jason. *How Fascism Works: The Politics of Us and Them.* New York: Random House, 2018.

Strossen, Nadine. *Hate. Why We Should Resist It with Free Speech, Not Censorship.* New York and Oxford: Oxford University Press, 2018.

Suarez-Orozco, Carola, and Marcelo Suarez-Orozco. *Transformations: Immigration, Family Life, and Achievement Motivation Among Latino Adolescents.* Stanford, CA: Stanford University Press, 1995.

Suk, Julie. Podcast Interview. *Think About It* podcast. July 3, 2018.

Thelin, John R. *A History of American Higher Education.* Baltimore: Johns Hopkins University Press, 2004.

Tseng-Putterman, Mark. "Asian-Americans, Diversity, and Campus Debates." Interview on *Think About It,* www.ulrichbaer.com, February 1, 2019.

Waldron, Jeremy. *The Harm in Hate Speech.* Cambridge, MA: Harvard University Press, 2012.

Wang, Amy. "One Group Loved Trump's Remarks about Charlottesville: White Supremacists." *Washington Post,* August 13, 2017.

Warikoo, Natasha K. *The Diversity Bargain: And Other Dilemmas of Race, Admissions, and Meritocracy at Elite Universities.* Chicago: University of Chicago, 2016.

Weil, Simone. *The Need for Roots: Prelude to a Declaration of Duties Towards Mankind.* New York: Routledge Classics, 2001.

Whittaker, Nicholas. "At the Heart of a Speech Controversy." Interview on *Think About It*, www.ulrichbaer.com, October 8, 2019.

Williams, Susan. *Truth, Autonomy and Speech.* New York: New York University Press, 2001.

Wood, Gordon. *Empire of Liberty. A History of the Early Republic.* Oxford: Oxford University Press, 2011. [First published 2009]

[Woodward, C. Vann] Report of the Committee on Freedom of Expression at Yale, 1973.

Zimmermann, Jonathan. *Campus Politics. What Everyone Needs to Know.* Oxford: Oxford University Press, 2017.

INDEX

New York Times v. Sullivan, 24–25
Nichols, Tom, xx–xxi
non-academic settings. *See*
    public sphere
Notre Dame, 109–11
Nunes, Devin, 26–27

Obama, Barack, 16–17
    on absolute free speech, 114
    current status quo and, 34
    Mexico City policy and, 109–11
    on racism, 59
offensive speech. *See* hate speech
Ohio State, 132–33
On Liberty (Mill), 82–83
open-carry states, 58–59
open inquiry. *See* academic
    freedom
opportunism, First Amendment,
    15–16, 149–50

pathos, 115–16
Penn State, 132–33
personal experience, 92–94
    authority *vs.,* 147
    gender and, 42
    privilege and, 93
    racism and, 42
    of silencing, 47
    teaching and, 161–62
    truth and, 147
Plato, 147–49, 152–54, 164–66
    on absolute free speech, 32
    suspicion of expertise and, 18
    on truth and politics, 19–20
police, filming of, x–xi
political correctness, x–xi
    as false framework, 5–7
    freedom of expression and, 1–2
    groupthink and, 19–20, 23–24
    regulation of speech and, 142
political polarization, 101–2

political speech
    alt-Right movement and, 60
    hate speech and, 61–62
    impact of, xvi–xvii
positivist legalistic view, 32
Post, Robert, 28–29, 89–90,
    129–30, 149–50
Postmodern Condition, The
    (Lyotard), 93
power, xii–xiii
    classroom participation
        and, 17–18
    dependence of students
        and, 7–8
    First Amendment and, 159–60
    force and, 152
    Founding Fathers on, xxi
    gatekeeping and, 22
    hate speech and, 61
    Skokie free speech case and, 62
    truth and, 19–20
    vetting of ideas and, 12–13
press
    coverage by, xvi–xvii
    freedom of, 159–60, 166–67
    independence of, xviii–xix
    Donald Trump and, 98
    vetting of ideas and, 35
privilege
    gender and, 48–49
    personal experience and, 93
    racism and, 48–49
progressives. *See* liberal/
    conservative alliance;
    liberalism
protest, 98
    equal participation and,
        105–6
    expulsion due to, 35–36, 68
    free speech and, x–xi
    racism and, 119–20, 146
    against speakers, 94